SCHOLASTIC

Morning Jumpstarts: Math

100 Independent Practice Pages to Build Essential Skills

Marcia Miller & Martin Lee

New York · Toronto · London · Auckland · Sydney
Mexico City · New Delhi · Hong Kong · Buenos Aires

Teaching *Resources*

Cover design by Scott Davis
Interior design by Melinda Belter
Interior illustrations by Teresa Anderko, Paige Billin-Frye, Melinda Belter,
Maxie Chambliss, Rusty Fletcher, and Anne Kennedy; © 2013 by Scholastic Inc.

Image credit, page 90: © Veniamin Kraskov/Shutterstock

978-0-545-46416-1

Copyright © 2013 by Scholastic Inc.

All rights reserved.
Printed in the U.S.A.
Published by Scholastic Inc.

2 3 4 5 6 7 8 9 10   40   20 19 18 17 16 15 14

Contents

Introduction 4

How to Use This Book 5

A Look Inside 6

Connections to the Common Core State Standards 7

Jumpstarts 1–50 9

Answers 109

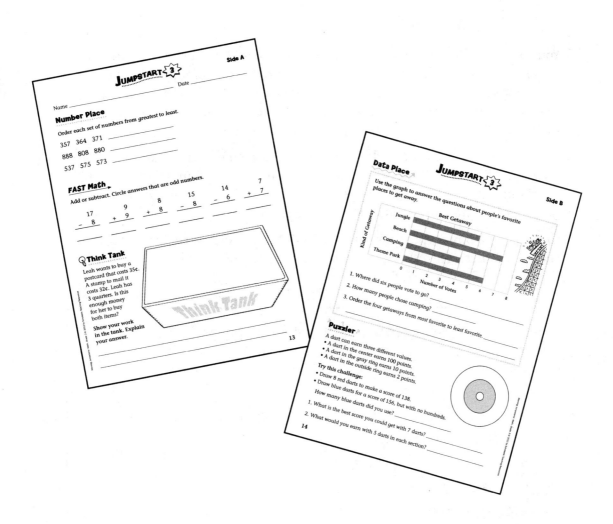

Introduction

In your busy classroom, you know how vital it is to energize students for the tasks of the day. That's why *Morning Jumpstarts: Math, Grade 3* is the perfect tool for you.

The activities in this book provide brief and focused individual practice on grade-level skills students are expected to master. Each Jumpstart is a two-page collection of five activities designed to review and reinforce a range of math skills and concepts students will build throughout the year. The consistent format helps students work independently and with confidence. Each Jumpstart includes these features:

- Number Place
- Data Place
- Fast Math
- Puzzler
- Think Tank

You can use a Jumpstart in its entirety or, because each feature is self-contained, assign sections at different times of the day or to different groups of learners. The Jumpstart activities will familiarize students with the kinds of challenges they will encounter on standardized tests, and provide review of skills they need to master. (See page 6 for a close-up look at the features in each Jumpstart.)

The Common Core State Standards (CCSS) for Mathematics serve as the backbone of the activities in this book. On pages 7–8, you'll find a correlation chart that details how the 50 Jumpstarts dovetail with the widely accepted set of guidelines for preparing students to succeed in math.

Generally, we have kept in mind the eight CCSS "mathematical practices" that should inform solid math exploration, calculation, and interpretation, even for the youngest learners.

Mathematical Practices

1. Make sense of problems and persevere in solving them.
2. Reason abstractly and quantitatively.
3. Construct viable arguments and critique the reasoning of others.
4. Model with mathematics.
5. Use appropriate tools strategically.
6. Attend to precision.
7. Look for and make use of structure.
8. Look for and express regularity in repeated reasoning.

Morning Jumpstarts: Math, Grade 3 © 2013 by Scholastic Teaching Resources

How to Use This Book

Morning Jumpstarts: Math, Grade 3 can be used in many ways—and not just in the morning! You know your students best, so feel free to pick and choose among the activities, and incorporate those as you see fit. You can make double-sided copies, or print one side at a time and staple the pages together.

We suggest the following times to present Jumpstarts:

- At the start of the school day, as a way to help children settle into the day's routines.
- Before lunch, as children ready themselves for their midday break.
- After lunch, as a calming transition into the afternoon's plans.
- Toward the end of the day, before children gather their belongings to go home, or as homework.

In general, the Jumpstarts progress in difficulty level and build on skills covered in previous sheets. Preview each one before you assign it to ensure that students have the skills needed to complete them. Keep in mind, however, that you may opt for some students to skip sections, as appropriate, or complete them together at a later time as part of a small-group or whole-class lesson.

Undoubtedly, students will complete their Jumpstart activity pages at different rates. We suggest that you set up a "what to do when I'm done" plan to give students who need more time a chance to finish without interruption. For example, you might encourage students to complete another Jumpstart or get started on a math homework assignment.

An answer key begins on page 109. You might want to review answers with the whole class. This approach provides opportunities for discussion, comparison, extension, reinforcement, and correlation to other skills and lessons in your current plans. Your observations can direct the kinds of review or reinforcement you may want to add to your lessons. Alternatively, you may find that having students discuss activity solutions and strategies in small groups is another effective approach.

When you introduce the first Jumpstart, walk through its sections with your class to provide an overview before you assign it and to make sure students understand the directions. Help students see that the activities in each section focus on different kinds of skills, and let them know that the same sections will repeat throughout each Jumpstart, always in the same order and position. You might want to work through the first few Jumpstarts as a group until students are comfortable with the routine and ready to work independently.

You know best how to assign the work to the students in your class. You might, for instance, stretch a Jumpstart over two days, assigning Side A on the first day and Side B on the second. Although the activities on different Jumpstarts vary in difficulty and in time needed, we anticipate that once students are familiar with the routine, most will be able to complete both sides of a Jumpstart in anywhere from 10 to 20 minutes.

A Look Inside

Each two-page Jumpstart includes the following skill-building features.

Number Place The first feature on Side A reviews grade-appropriate place-value skills related to whole numbers, decimals, fractions, and integers. Regardless of the particular presentation, students will use their knowledge of place value and their number sense to complete this feature. A solid place-value foundation is essential for success with computation and estimation, and for an overall grasp of numerical patterns and relationships.

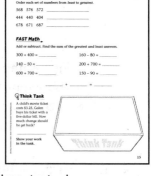

Fast Math The second Side A feature addresses necessary grade-level computation skills with the goal of building automaticity, fluency, and accuracy. To work through these exercises, students draw upon their understanding of computation strategies and mathematical properties. In some instances, students will review skills that have been covered previously. This is a good way to keep math skills sharp and to point out to you where revisiting a skill or algorithm may be beneficial.

Think Tank This feature rounds out side A by offering an original word problem that draws from a wide spectrum of grade-appropriate skills, strategies, and approaches. Some are single-step problems; others require multiple steps to solve. The think tank itself provides a place where students can draw, do computations, and work out their thinking. This is a particularly good section to discuss together, to share solutions, as well as to compare and contrast approaches and strategies. Encourage students to recognize that many problems can be solved in more than one way, or may have more than one solution.

Data Place Every Side B begins with an activity in which students solve problems based on reading, collecting, representing, and interpreting data that is presented in many formats: lists, tables, charts, pictures, and, mostly, in a variety of graphs. In our rapidly changing world, it is essential that students build visual literacy by becoming familiar with many kinds of graphic presentations. This feature presents the kinds of graphs students are likely to encounter online, on TV, and in newspapers and magazines. Many include data from other curriculum areas.

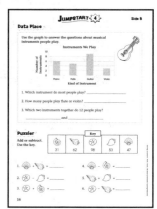

Puzzler Side B always ends with some form of an entertaining challenge: a brainteaser, puzzle, non-routine problem, code, or other engaging task designed to stretch the mind. While some children may find this section particularly challenging, others will relish teasing out trick solutions. This feature provides another chance for group work or discussion. It may prove useful to invite pairs of children to tackle these exercises together. And, when appropriate, invite children to create their own challenges, using ideas sparked by these exercises. Feel free to create your own variations of any brainteasers your class enjoys.

Morning Jumpstarts: Math, Grade 3 © 2013 by Scholastic Teaching Resources

Connections to the Common Core State Standards

As shown in the chart below and on page 8, the activities in this book will help you meet your specific state math standards as well as those outlined in the CCSS. These materials address the following standards for students in grade 3. For details on these standards, visit the CCSS Web site: www.corestandards.org/the-standards/.

JS	3.OA.1	3.OA.2	3.OA.3	3.OA.4	3.OA.5	3.OA.6	3.OA.7	3.OA.8	3.OA.9	3.NBT.1	3.NBT.2	3.NBT.3	3.NF.1	3.NF.2	3.NF.3	3.MD.1	3.MD.2	3.MD.3	3.MD.5	3.MD.6	3.MD.7	3.MD.8	3.G.1	3.G.2
			Operations & Algebraic Thinking							Number & Operations in Base Ten			Number & Operations —Fractions			Measurement & Data							Geometry	
1								●	●		●							●						
2								●	●		●							●						
3	●		●					●	●		●	●						●						
4								●	●		●							●						
5								●	●		●							●					●	
6	●		●				●	●	●		●							●					●	
7								●	●		●					●		●					●	
8								●	●		●							●						
9								●	●	●	●							●					●	
10	●		●	●			●	●	●	●	●							●						
11			●	●				●	●	●	●							●				●		
12								●	●	●	●							●						
13								●			●					●		●						
14	●		●					●	●	●	●							●			●			
15	●	●	●				●	●			●							●						
16								●			●							●					●	
17								●			●							●			●			
18								●		●	●		●		●	●		●	●	●			●	
19								●	●	●	●							●			●			
20	●		●				●	●	●	●	●	●						●						
21	●		●				●	●	●	●	●							●						
22	●		●	●			●	●	●	●	●							●						
23	●		●	●			●	●	●		●							●						
24	●		●	●			●	●	●		●							●	●	●	●			
25	●		●	●	●		●	●	●									●				●		

Morning Jumpstarts: Math, Grade 3 © 2013 by Scholastic Teaching Resources

Connections to the Common Core State Standards

JS	Operations & Algebraic Thinking									Number & Operations in Base Ten			Number & Operations—Fractions			Measurement & Data							Geometry	
	3.OA.1	3.OA.2	3.OA.3	3.OA.4	3.OA.5	3.OA.6	3.OA.7	3.OA.8	3.OA.9	3.NBT.1	3.NBT.2	3.NBT.3	3.NF.1	3.NF.2	3.NF.3	3.MD.1	3.MD.2	3.MD.3	3.MD.5	3.MD.6	3.MD.7	3.MD.8	3.G.1	3.G.2
26	•		•	•	•		•	•	•		•	•						•	•	•	•	•		
27	•		•	•	•			•	•		•		•					•						•
28		•	•	•		•	•	•					•		•			•						
29		•	•	•		•	•				•		•		•			•						
30		•	•	•			•	•			•							•						
31	•	•	•	•			•	•	•		•	•						•						
32	•		•	•			•	•	•	•	•		•		•			•						•
33		•	•	•	•		•	•	•	•	•		•				•	•						
34	•				•		•	•	•		•		•					•						
35	•		•	•	•		•	•	•		•							•						
36	•		•				•	•	•		•	•					•	•	•	•	•			
37						•				•	•		•		•			•						
38						•	•	•			•		•		•	•		•						
39	•			•		•	•	•		•	•		•		•	•		•					•	•
40				•			•	•			•		•		•			•					•	•
41						•					•		•	•	•			•						
42	•	•	•	•	•	•	•	•	•		•		•		•			•						
43	•	•	•	•	•	•	•	•			•		•		•			•						•
44	•		•	•	•	•	•	•	•	•	•		•		•			•						•
45							•				•		•		•		•	•					•	
46							•	•	•	•	•		•		•			•						
47				•			•	•	•	•								•						
48			•	•		•	•											•						•
49			•	•		•	•	•								•		•	•	•			•	
50			•	•	•		•						•		•	•		•						•

Morning Jumpstarts: Math, Grade 3 © 2013 by Scholastic Teaching Resources

Name _____ Date _____

Number Place

Write the number that is 10 *more*.

22 _____   55 _____   87 _____

203 _____   661 _____   919 _____

Write the number that is 10 *less*.

23 _____   79 _____   96 _____

834 _____   545 _____   714 _____

FAST Math

Add or subtract. Circle any answer that is your age.

$4 + 7 =$ _____ $11 - 6 =$ _____ $8 - 7 =$ _____

$3 + 5 =$ _____ $6 + 5 =$ _____ $12 - 3 =$ _____

$7 + 5 =$ _____ $12 - 5 =$ _____ $11 - 4 =$ _____

Think Tank

Jen has fewer pets than Kai. Kai has more pets than Dan. Dan has more pets than Jen, but fewer pets than Rosa. Who has the fewest pets?

_____

Show your work in the tank.

Data Place

Count and tally the music symbols in the table below.

Music Symbols

Symbol	Tallies
Sharp ♯	
Flat ♭	
Note ♪	

1. How many notes? _____

2. How many music symbols in all? _____

Puzzler

Count *back* from 93 to connect the dots.

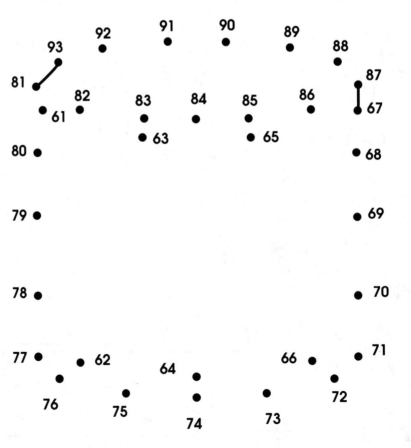

Name _____ Date _____

Number Place

Write the number that is 100 *more*.

67 _____   80 _____   93 _____

356 _____   518 _____   747 _____

Write the number that is 100 *less*.

212 _____   605 _____   999 _____

184 _____   461 _____   826 _____

FAST Math ▶

Add or subtract. Circle any answer if it matches today's date.

$9 + 8 =$ _____ $16 - 9 =$ _____ $18 - 9 =$ _____

$7 + 8 =$ _____ $8 + 5 =$ _____ $15 - 7 =$ _____

$5 + 9 =$ _____ $20 - 10 =$ _____ $14 - 8 =$ _____

💡 Think Tank

Read the sentence in the tank. What is the 10th word?

_____

What is the 35th letter?

_____

Explain how you found the answers.

_____

_____

The first skateboard was probably made by nailing skate wheels onto a board.

Think Tank

Data Place

The table shows some items sold at a fishing shop.

Use the data to answer the questions.

Item	Number Sold
Bait Bucket	8
Fishing Line	31
Rod & Reel	17
Tackle Box	24

1. How many tackle boxes were sold?

   _____

2. Which item sold the most?

   _____

3. Which item sold about twice as many as the bait bucket did?

   _____

Puzzler

A magic square is an ancient math puzzle. The Chinese first made the puzzle over 2,600 years ago.

Write the digits 1–9 _once_ each in the blank boxes of the square. The sum of each row, column, and diagonal must be 15. Three of the digits are already in place. Figure out where to place the rest of them.

Explain your solution method.

8		
	5	
4		

_____

_____

_____

Morning Jumpstarts: Math, Grade 3 © 2013 by Scholastic Teaching Resources

Name _____ Date _____

Number Place

Order each set of numbers from *greatest* to *least*.

357 364 371 _____

888 808 880 _____

537 575 573 _____

FAST Math ▸

Add or subtract. Circle answers that are *odd* numbers.

17	9	8	15	14	7
− 8	+ 9	+ 8	− 8	− 6	+ 7

_____ _____ _____ _____ _____ _____

💡 Think Tank

Leah wants to buy a postcard that costs 35¢. A stamp to mail it costs 32¢. Leah has 3 quarters. Is this enough money for her to buy both items?

Show your work in the tank. Explain your answer.

_____

_____

Data Place

Use the graph to answer the questions about people's favorite places to get away.

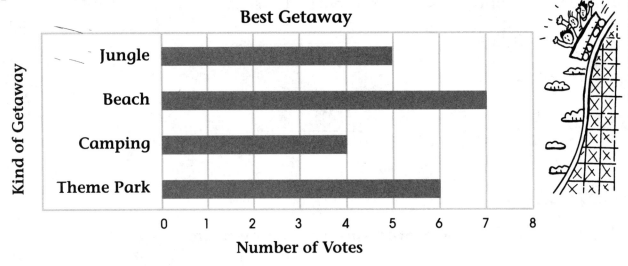

1. Where did 6 people vote to go? _____

2. How many people chose camping? _____

3. Order the four getaways from *most* favorite to *least* favorite. _____

_____

Puzzler

A dart can earn 3 different values.
- A dart in the center earns 100 points.
- A dart in the gray ring earns 10 points.
- A dart in the outside ring earns 2 points.

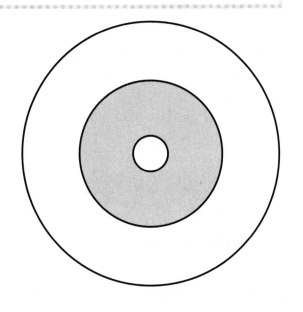

1. What is the best score you could get

   with 7 darts? _____

2. What would you earn with 5 darts

   in each section? _____

3. Draw 8 darts to make a score of 138.

14

Name _____ Date _____

Number Place

Order each set of numbers from *least* to *greatest*.

568 576 572 _____

444 440 404 _____

678 671 687 _____

FAST Math ▶

Add or subtract. Find the sum of the *greatest* and *least* answers.

300 + 400 = _____   160 – 80 = _____

140 – 50 = _____   200 + 700 = _____

600 + 700 = _____   150 – 90 = _____

_____ + _____ = _____

💡 Think Tank

A child's movie ticket costs $3.25. Galen buys his ticket with a five-dollar bill. How much change should he get back?

_____

Show your work in the tank.

Data Place

Use the graph to answer the questions about musical instruments people play.

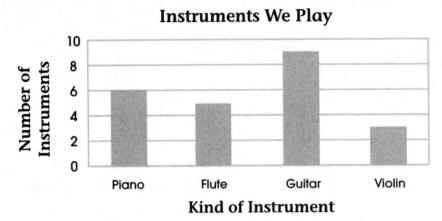

Instruments We Play

1. Which instrument do most people play? _____

2. How many people play flute or violin? _____

3. Which 2 instruments together do 12 people play?

   _____ and _____

Puzzler

Add or subtract.
Use the key.

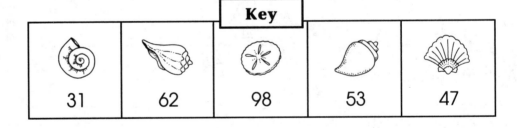

Key				
31	62	98	53	47

1. 🐚 + 🐚 = _____

2. 🐚 – 🐚 = _____

3. 🐚 + 🐚 = _____

4. 🐚 – 🐚 = _____

5. 🐚 + 🐚 = _____

6. 🐚 – 🐚 = _____

Morning Jumpstarts: Math, Grade 3 © 2013 by Scholastic Teaching Resources

Name _____ Date _____

Number Place

Write the missing numbers.

109, _____ , _____ , _____ , _____ , 114

318, _____ , _____ , _____ , _____ , 323

767, _____ , _____ , _____ , _____ , 772

FAST Math ▶

Is each number in the mitten *odd* or *even*?
Write each number where it belongs.

Odd Numbers	Even Numbers

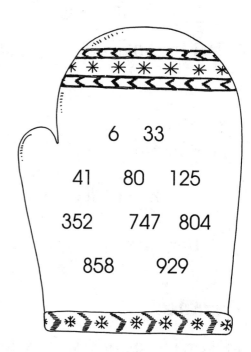

6   33

41   80   125

352   747   804

858   929

💡 Think Tank

Frank is third in a line of 8 boys. Kent is right behind Frank. Next are José and Alvy. How many boys are lined up behind Alvy?

_____

Draw a picture in the tank.

Morning Jumpstarts: Math, Grade 3 © 2013 by Scholastic Teaching Resources

Data Place

Use the graph to answer the questions about animals people think are most scary.

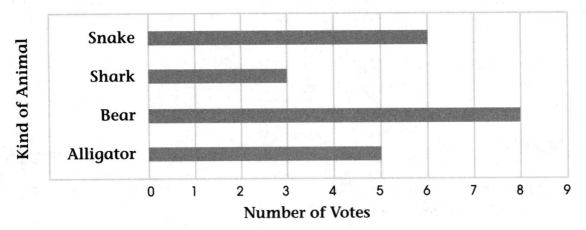

Scariest Animal

Kind of Animal: Snake, Shark, Bear, Alligator

Number of Votes

1. How many people voted in the survey? _____

2. Which animal was voted the scariest? _____

3. How many more people fear snakes than sharks? _____

Puzzler

Make a picture or design using *only* the shapes at right. You may vary the sizes. Use every shape at least twice.

Morning Jumpstarts: Math, Grade 3 © 2013 by Scholastic Teaching Resources

Name _____ Date _____

Number Place

Use every number in the box just *once*.

35 > _____   61 > _____

13 < _____   50 < _____

_____ < _____

26	55
30	74
69	18

FAST Math →

Write two numbers to fit each rule.

- even numbers between 50 and 55   _____ and _____

- *odd* numbers closest to 90   _____ and _____

- *odd* numbers between 114 and 119   _____ and _____

- *even* numbers greater than 620   _____ and _____

💡 Think Tank

Use the menu. How much would you pay in all for the cheapest food and most expensive drink?

Show your work in the tank. Explain your thinking.

MENU

Hot Dog . . $1.19	Juice . . . $1.09
Burger $1.79	Soda . . . $1.20
Taco $1.33	Milk . . . . . $ .60
Egg Roll . . $1.49	Tea . . . . . $ .55

Think Tank

_____

_____

_____

_____

Data Place

Use the graph to answer the questions about sports third graders play.

Sports Third Graders Play

Baseball	○ ○ ○ ○ ○
Basketball	○
Football	○ ○
Hockey	○ ○ ○
Soccer	○ ○ ○ ○ ○ ○ ○

Key: ○ = 5 students

1. What does the key show? _____

2. Which sport do 5 students play? _____

3. What might make soccer the most popular sport? _____

_____

Puzzler

Using 13 toothpicks,
make 4 squares as shown.
Then take away 1 toothpick
to leave only 3 squares.

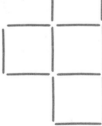

Explain how you solved this puzzle.

_____

_____

_____

Morning Jumpstarts: Math, Grade 3 © 2013 by Scholastic Teaching Resources

Name _____ Date _____

Number Place

Label the columns on the place-value chart below from *Ones* to *Thousands*.
Then write *two thousand, one hundred sixty-one* in number form.

FAST Math

Write the time for each clock. **X** a time when school may start.

_____   _____   _____   _____

💡 Think Tank

Captain Karl has
32 sailboats and
27 rowboats to rent.
Today he rented
46 boats. How many
boats were *not* rented?

_____

**Show your work
in the tank.**

Data Place

A class made a frequency table about pets.

Finish the table. Then answer the questions.

How Many Pets Live with You?

Range	Tallies	Number
0	⫴⫴⫴ I	
1-2		8
3-5	IIII	
6-8	⫴⫴⫴	
9 or more		3

1. How many homes have no pets? _____

2. How many homes have fewer than 9 pets? _____

3. Roy has 14 pets. If he added his data to the table, what would change?

_____

Puzzler

Use the numbers in the figure to solve the problems below.

Find the sum of numbers:

- *not* inside the oval or triangle _____

- inside the triangle *only* _____

- inside the oval *only* _____

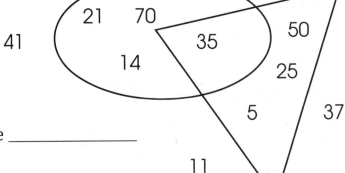

Morning Jumpstarts: Math, Grade 3 © 2013 by Scholastic Teaching Resources

Name _____ Date _____

Number Place

Write the number that comes just *before*.	Write the number that comes just *after*.

_____ , 600   399, _____

_____ , 900   799, _____

_____ , 100   999, _____

FAST Math ▶

Skip count. Write the missing numbers in each row.

30, 32, 34, _____ , _____ , _____ , 42, _____

63, 66, 69, _____ , _____ , 78, _____ , _____

_____ , 50, 55, _____ , _____ , 70, _____

💡 Think Tank

A pizza cart offers 4 toppings and 3 types of crusts. How many *different* pizzas could be made using 1 topping and 1 type of crust?

_____

TOPPINGS	CRUSTS
Mushrooms	Regular
Olives	Super Thin
Pepperoni	Whole Wheat
Sausage	

Make a list or diagram the choices in the tank.

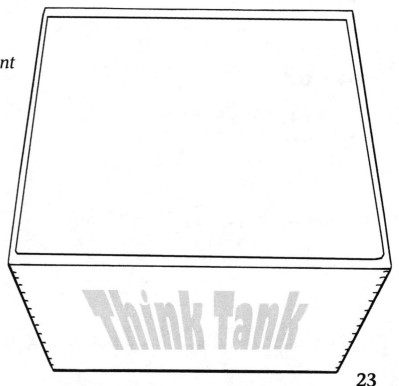

Data Place

Draw each point on the coordinate grid.
Then connect the points in order to make a closed figure.

$$(4, 1) \rightarrow (2, 0) \rightarrow (0, 2) \rightarrow (2, 3) \rightarrow (4, 1)$$

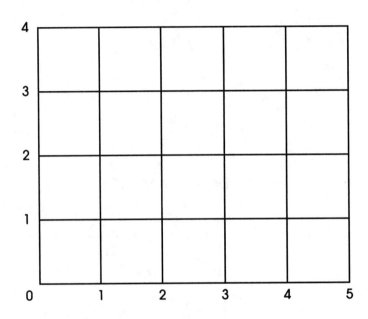

Describe the shape you made. _____

_____

Puzzler

How many triangles are there
in this figure?

_____

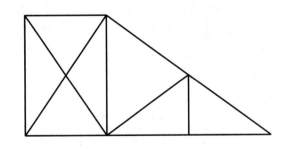

How did you organize your thinking?

_____

_____

_____

Morning Jumpstarts: Math, Grade 3 © 2013 by Scholastic Teaching Resources

Name _____ Date _____

Number Place

Round each number to the nearest ten.

64 → _____   87 → _____   215 → _____

372 → _____   549 → _____   806 → _____

FAST Math

Skip count. Write the missing numbers in each row.

0, 6, 12, _____ , _____ , 30, _____ , 42, _____

24, 28, _____ , _____ , 40, _____ , _____ , 52

_____ , 18, 27, 36, _____ , _____ , _____ , 70

Think Tank

Figure out the pattern. Draw what comes next.

Data Place

The table shows the number of students in different after-school clubs.

Club	Students
Arts & Crafts	27
Computer	44
Cooking	17
Science Lab	23
Yoga for Kids	9

Use the data to answer the questions.

1. How many clubs are there? _____

2. Which clubs have around 20 members? _____

_____

3. Which 2 clubs together have as many members as the computer

club does? _____

Puzzler

Use the clues below to fill in the secret word.
It names a real place in Pennsylvania.

____ ____ ____ ____ ____ ____ ____ ____ ____ ____

The seventh letter is *t*.   The ninth letter is *w*.
The second letter is *h*.   The first letter is *c*.
The fifth letter is *s*.   The eighth letter is *o*.
The tenth letter is *n*.   The third, fourth, and sixth letters are *e*.

Morning Jumpstarts: Math, Grade 3 © 2013 by Scholastic Teaching Resources

Name _____ Date _____

Number Place

Round each number to the nearest hundred.

138 ⟶ _____   862 ⟶ _____   447 ⟶ _____

671 ⟶ _____   254 ⟶ _____   906 ⟶ _____

FAST Math

Skip count. Write the missing numbers in each row.

7, 14, 21, _____ , _____ , 42, _____ , _____

_____ , 24, 32, _____ , _____ , 56, _____ , 72

_____ , 22, 33, 44, _____ , _____ , 77, _____

💡 Think Tank

Tamar found 14 Web sites that have photos of Mars. Jay found 6 of those sites and 5 others that Tamar did not find. How many different Web sites did they find in all?

Show your work in the tank. Explain your thinking.

_____

_____

Data Place

The line plot shows how many spots students counted on different ladybugs they saw on a science walk.

Use the data to answer the questions.

Spots on Ladybugs

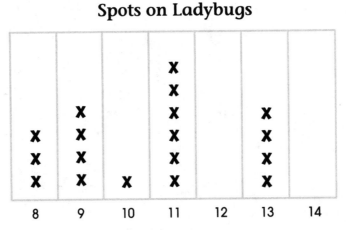

1. How many ladybugs did the students count? _____

2. How many ladybugs had 11 spots? _____

3. How many ladybugs had fewer than 10 spots? _____

4. How many 12-spot ladybugs did the students count? _____

Puzzler

Paco has only 3¢ stamps and 5¢ stamps. He can use any mix of them for postage.

For example, if Paco needs 16¢ postage, he can use two 5¢ stamps and two 3¢ stamps. But two amounts between 3¢ and 25¢ are *impossible* to make. What amounts are they?

Hint: Make an organized list.

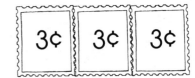

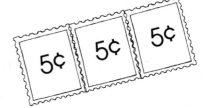

_____

_____

Morning Jumpstarts: Math, Grade 3 © 2013 by Scholastic Teaching Resources

JUMPSTART 11

Side A

Name _____ Date _____

Number Place

Write <, =, or >.

794 ◯ 749   818 ◯ 798   ninety ◯ 90

20 tens ◯ 199   500 + 60 ◯ 600 + 50

FAST Math

Add or subtract. Circle answers that are *even* numbers.

20	9	2	16	13	8
− 15	+ 9	+ 9	− 7	− 5	+ 9

💡 Think Tank

Randy made a banner for his team. It is shaped liked a triangle. Each side of the banner is 42 inches long. How many inches is it around Randy's team banner?

_____

Draw a picture in the tank to show your work.

Morning Jumpstarts: Math, Grade 3 © 2013 by Scholastic Teaching Resources

29

JUMPSTART 11

Data Place

Use the data in the calendar to answer the questions.

1. Two dates in a row have a sum of 29. What are the dates?

   _____

2. Three dates in a row have a sum of 12. What are the dates?

   _____

NOVEMBER

SUN	MON	TUE	WED	THU	FRI	SAT
		1	2	3	4	5
6	7	8	9	10	11	12
13	14	15	16	17	18	19
20	21	22	23	24	25	26
27	28	29	30			

3. What is the sum of dates on the first 3 Sundays? _____

4. Thanksgiving falls on the 4th Thursday of November.

   What is its date? _____

Puzzler

Figure out each code. Fill in the blanks.

1. 🐜 + 🦋 = 5 and 🦋 + 🐞 = 9.

   If 🐜 = 3, then 🦋 = _____ and 🐞 = _____ .

2. 🍎 + 🍎 = 🍓 and 🍓 + 🍒 = 11.

   If 🍒 = 5, then 🍓 = _____ and 🍎 = _____ .

Name _____ Date _____

Number Place

Write each number in expanded form.

863 _____

907 _____

4,152 _____

two-thousand twelve _____

FAST Math ▸

Find each sum. Circle the answer whose digits add to 21.

203	526	447	749	160	813
+ 154	+ 253	+ 231	+ 130	+ 629	+ 145
_____	_____	_____	_____	_____	_____

💡 Think Tank

California has some HUGE trees. The Hyperion redwood, at 379 feet high, is the world's tallest living tree. The General Sherman sequoia is 275 feet tall. Its trunk is so thick that scientists call it the largest tree in the world. Find the difference in their heights.

_____

Show your work in the tank.

Data Place

Each student in Mr. Kim's science class voted for a favorite planet.

Use the data in the table to answer the questions.

Planet	Votes
Mercury	2
Venus	3
Earth	7
Mars	4
Jupiter	5
Saturn	3
Uranus	0
Neptune	2

1. Which planets got the same number of votes?

   Explain. _____

   _____

2. Why do you think Earth got the most votes?

   _____

3. How many votes were cast in all? _____

Puzzler

The grid has hidden addition and subtraction facts.
Some are horizontal ⟷ . Others are vertical ↕ .
Some facts may overlap. Two have been done as examples

Circle every fact you find.

11	8	3	5	9	14	0	16	8
9	4	13	5	8	13	10	8	7
2	3	7	10	11	9	6	8	9
18	9	9	6	3	4	5	9	16
7	9	16	4	8	12	11	17	4

Morning Jumpstarts: Math, Grade 3 © 2013 by Scholastic Teaching Resources

Name _____ Date _____

Number Place

Write each number in word form.

1,296 _____

8,075 _____

3,364 _____

24,689 _____

FAST Math

Subtract. Circle the *greatest* answer.

725	948	539	678	876	450
− 301	− 235	− 427	− 432	− 254	− 230

_____ _____ _____ _____ _____ _____

💡 Think Tank

The 3 longest sharks are the whale shark, the basking shark, and the great white shark. Read their lengths in the Think Tank. If all 3 sharks swam end to end, what would their total length be?

_____

Show your work in the tank.

Whale Shark: 41 feet

Basking Shark: 40 feet

Great White Shark: 26 feet

Think Tank

Data Place

Ms. DiMeo posts a class schedule each morning. It shows what will happen during the school day.

Use the schedule to answer the questions.

1. What happens between the end of one subject and the start of the next one? Why might this be?

_____

_____

Subject	Start	End
Class Meeting	8:50 A.M.	9:05 A.M.
Math	9:10 A.M.	9:55 A.M.
Social Studies	10:00 A.M.	10:45 A.M.
Gym	10:50 A.M.	11:35 A.M.
Lunch & Recess	11:40 A.M.	12:25 P.M.
Reading	12:30 P.M.	1:40 P.M.
Science	1:45 P.M.	2:25 P.M.
Music	2:30 P.M.	2:55 P.M.

2. Which subject starts in the morning and ends in the afternoon?

_____

3. Which subject gets the longest time slot? The shortest?

_____

Puzzler

Each letter has a number value. Use the code to find the value of each word.

A = 1	B = 2	C = 3	D = 4	E = 5	F = 6	G = 7
H = 8	I = 9	J = 10	K = 11	L = 12	M = 13	N = 14
O = 15	P = 16	Q = 17	R = 18	S = 19	T = 20	U = 21
V = 22	W = 23	X = 24	Y = 25	Z = 26		

1. ink _____   3. yak _____   5. jeep _____

2. box _____   4. good _____   6. zebra _____

Morning Jumpstarts: Math, Grade 3 © 2013 by Scholastic Teaching Resources

Name _____ Date _____

Number Place

Solve the riddle about a 3-digit number.

- I round to 900.

- I have twice as many hundreds as ones.

- All my digits are different, but their sum is 18.

> The number is
>
> _____ .

FAST Math

Add. Regroup as needed. Circle the *least* answer.

$$\begin{array}{r} 48 \\ +\ 49 \\ \hline \end{array} \qquad \begin{array}{r} 53 \\ +\ 28 \\ \hline \end{array} \qquad \begin{array}{r} 687 \\ +\ 252 \\ \hline \end{array} \qquad \begin{array}{r} 308 \\ +\ 951 \\ \hline \end{array} \qquad \begin{array}{r} 545 \\ +\ 194 \\ \hline \end{array} \qquad \begin{array}{r} 436 \\ +\ 743 \\ \hline \end{array}$$

Think Tank

Twyla makes friendship bracelets with cording and clay beads. She uses 9 beads for each bracelet. How many beads will Twyla need to make 5 bracelets?

_____

Draw a picture in the tank to show your work. Explain your thinking.

_____

_____

Morning Jumpstarts: Math, Grade 3 © 2013 by Scholastic Teaching Resources

Data Place

Hallie's class runs a small school supply shop. They sell the items shown in the table.

Use the table to answer the questions.

1. How much to buy 10 pencils?

   _____

2. How much to buy 2 rulers?

   _____

3. Which costs more: 3 erasers or 1 marker?

   _____

   How much more? _____

4. One glue stick costs about the same as _____ pencils.

Item		Cost
Pencil		$.10
Eraser		$.35
Marker		$1.09
Ruler		$.49
Glue Stick		$.78

Puzzler

Andre stretched one rubber band to make a 5 on his geoboard.

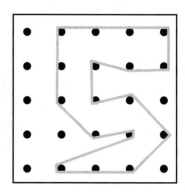

1. How many pins does the rubber band touch? _____

2. How many pins are *not* touched? _____

3. How many sides does the 5 have? _____

4. How many pins are on the whole geoboard? _____

JUMPSTART ⟨15⟩

Name _____ Date _____

Number Place

Write each money amount in the place-value chart.

Pig	Dollars	Dimes	Pennies
1			
2			
3			

Pig 1

Pig 2

Pig 3

FAST Math ▶

Subtract. Regroup as needed.
Circle the answer that has 1 ten.

93	61	527	809	415	633
− 46	− 37	− 108	− 547	− 165	− 590

_____   _____   _____   _____   _____   _____

💡 Think Tank

A lacrosse team needs 10 players. There are 43 kids who go to lacrosse camp. How many equal teams can be formed? Will everyone be on a team?

_____ _____

Show your work in the tank. Explain your thinking.

Morning Jumpstarts: Math, Grade 3 © 2013 by Scholastic Teaching Resources

Data Place

How many of each item in your classroom?

Count and tally. Then graph the results.

What's in Our Classroom?

Windows	
Doors	
Lights	
Computers	

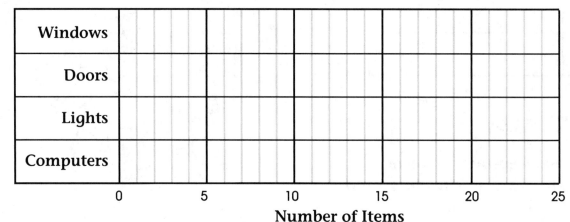

Kind of Item

Windows				
Doors				
Lights				
Computers				

0   5   10   15   20   25

Number of Items

What was hardest about this activity? _____

_____

_____

Puzzler

Each problem has some missing digits.
Each of the digits 0–9 is missing only *once*.

Use number sense to fill them in correctly.

```
  8 6 □        1 □ 3        □ 6 3        3 □ 5        □ 3 6
– □ 4 8      + 4 6 8      – 1 □ 9      + 5 1 □      – 2 7 □
───────      ───────      ───────      ───────      ───────
  5 1 8        5 9 □        6 5 4        9 0 0        6 6 2
```

38

Name _____ Date _____

Number Place

Rewrite each money amount. Use $ and .

42¢ is the same as _____ .

80¢ is the same as _____ .

11¢ is the same as _____ .

6¢ is the same as _____ .

FAST Math ▶

Add. Circle the sum that has 0 ones.

87	98	139	507	632	468
+ 96	+ 59	+ 589	+ 948	+ 298	+ 356
___	___	___	___	___	___

💡 Think Tank

Max is a bus driver. His route covers 400 miles. He drives 148 miles before lunch. He drives 161 miles after lunch, and then stops for gas. How many more miles are left in his route?

_____

Show your work in the tank.

Data Place

Make a Venn diagram. Write how you and a friend are alike in the overlapping part. Write how you are different in each separate part.

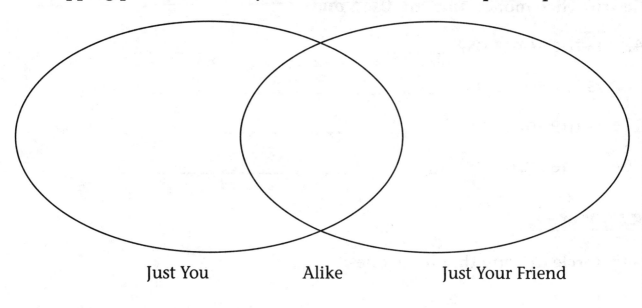

Just You   Alike   Just Your Friend

Puzzler

Fill in this design using 4 different colors. You can repeat colors—but not where sections touch.

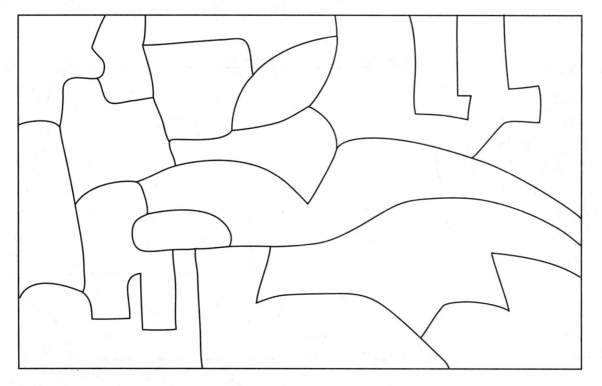

Morning Jumpstarts: Math, Grade 3 © 2013 by Scholastic Teaching Resources

Name _____ Date _____

Number Place

Rewrite each money amount. Use $ and .

137¢ is the same as _____ .

459¢ is the same as _____ .

600¢ is the same as _____ .

281¢ is the same as _____ .

FAST Math

Subtract. Circle two answers that have the same number of ones.

712	563	841	472	625	933
− 384	− 198	− 567	− 189	− 236	− 389
_____	_____	_____	_____	_____	_____

Think Tank

Dad is 37 years old. Mom is 5 years younger than he is. Mom is 22 years older than Taye. Taye is 3 years older than Femi. How old is Taye?

_____

How old is Femi?

_____

Show your work in the tank.

Data Place

Use the map to answer the questions.

1. Which town is nearest to Shrub?

   _____

2. How far is it from Maple to Elm and back again?

   _____

3. Which 2 towns are 30 miles apart?

   _____

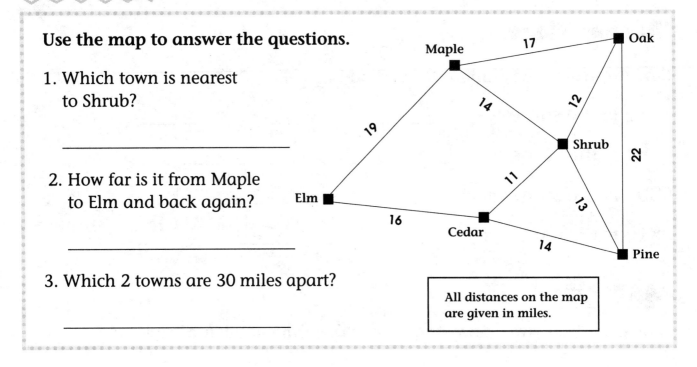

All distances on the map are given in miles.

Puzzler

Start at ☆. End at ✋. Add through exactly 8 squares to make the highest possible sum. You can move in any direction, but you can't use the same square twice. Can you beat 550?

☆	70	90	30	20	60
90	30	10	60	90	50
10	60	80	40	30	10
80	40	20	50	80	70
20	50	70	10	40	✋

Morning Jumpstarts: Math, Grade 3 © 2013 by Scholastic Teaching Resources

Name _____ Date _____

Number Place

Round each money amount to the nearest dime.

37¢ → _____   52¢ → _____   79¢ → _____

44¢ → _____   65¢ → _____   11¢ → _____

FAST Math

Subtract. Circle the 2-digit difference.

900	800	700	600	500	400
− 123	− 456	− 287	− 309	− 184	− 371

_____   _____   _____   _____   _____   _____

Think Tank

The Roths got to the park at 1:15 P.M. First they hiked with a ranger. Then they swam in the pool and had snacks. They left for home at 4:45 P.M. How long were the Roths at the park?

_____

Show your work in the tank. Explain your thinking.

_____

_____

Morning Jumpstarts: Math, Grade 3 © 2013 by Scholastic Teaching Resources

Data Place

Use the circle graph to answer the questions about students' after-school activities.

Students' After-School Activities

☐ Play Sports

▨ Take Lessons

▨ Go Home

■ Do Homework

1. What do the different sections tell? _____

_____

2. Which activity do about half the students do? _____

3. What is the least common activity? _____

Puzzler

Write how many rectangles this figure has in all. _____

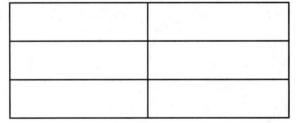

How did you organize your thinking?

_____

_____

_____

Morning Jumpstarts: Math, Grade 3 © 2013 by Scholastic Teaching Resources

Name _____ Date _____

Number Place

Round each money amount to the nearest dollar.

$1.17 → _____ $2.46 → _____ $3.50 → _____

$4.35 → _____ $5.09 → _____ $6.63 → _____

FAST Math

Add. Circle two sums that are the same.

25	67	39	531	807	668
80	18	44	708	426	109
+ 34	+ 52	+ 56	+ 226	+ 394	+ 951
_____	_____	_____	_____	_____	_____

Think Tank

Omar wants to build a dog run in his yard. It will be a rectangle, like the sketch. How many meters of fencing does he need to fence in the entire run?

_____

Show your work in the tank. Explain your thinking.

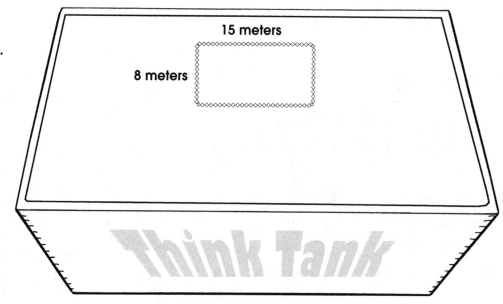

15 meters

8 meters

Think Tank

_____

_____

Data Place

Use the table to answer the questions about tickets for concert hall seats.

Seats in a Concert Hall

Location	Number	Price
Main Floor Center	175	$55
Main Floor Sides	62	$45
1st Balcony	116	$35
2nd Balcony	74	$20

1. Are there more seats on the main floor or in the balconies? _____

   How many more? _____

2. A family of 4 has $90 to spend on tickets.

   Which price ticket should they buy? _____

3. Ramon got 2 tickets for $110. Where are his seats? _____

   _____

Puzzler

Find a path through every white box *(only once)* without lifting your pencil.

Start and end at the sun. You may not go through the gray box.

Hint: Try with your finger first.

Morning Jumpstarts: Math, Grade 3 © 2013 by Scholastic Teaching Resources

Name _____ Date _____

Number Place

Write each money amount with $ and .

• nine dollars and seventy-five cents   _____

• three dollars and sixty cents   _____

• five dollars and three cents   _____

• eight dollars   _____

FAST Math ➤

Add. Circle the sum that rounds to 1,400.

54	687	853	428	593	3
317	12	251	78	8	907
+ 29	+ 304	+ 67	+ 906	+ 65	+ 56
_____	_____	_____	_____	_____	_____

💡 Think Tank

Ruby has $5 to buy art supplies. She wants 4 items on the list. Which 4 can she afford? How much does she spend?

ART SUPPLIES	
Clay	$ 1.75
Felt	$ .92
Glue	$ 1.67
Marker Set	$ 2.33
Paintbrush	$ .59

_____

_____

Show your work in the tank.

Data Place

Use the graph to answer the questions about people's favorite yogurt flavors.

Favorite Yogurt Flavors

Strawberry	🥤
Peach	🥤 🥤 🥤 🥤
Lemon	🥤
Vanilla	🥤 🥤 🥤

Key: 🥤 = 4 votes

1. What is the value of one 🥤 ? _____

2. How many people
   voted for lemon yogurt? _____ For peach yogurt? _____

3. What is the difference in number
   of votes between vanilla and strawberry? _____

Puzzler

You walk Mr. Tan's dog each morning for 7 days. He says, "I could pay you $10 a walk. Or I could pay you 1 dollar for the first walk, and double the amount for each walk after that." Which plan will you take?

Complete the table to help you decide.

Day	1	2	3	4	5	6	7
Dollars	1	2	4				

1. How much would you earn at $10 a walk? _____

2. How much would you earn the other way? _____

3. Would the doubling plan pay more than the $10 plan if
   Mr. Tan paid 50¢ for the first walk?

Explain. _____

48

Morning Jumpstarts: Math, Grade 3 © 2013 by Scholastic Teaching Resources

Name _____ Date _____

Number Place

Round each number to the nearest ten and hundred.

Number	Nearest 10	Nearest 100
919		
862		
345		

FAST Math

Use mental math to estimate each answer.

271 + 328 → _____   835 – 694 → _____

939 – 554 → _____   309 + 117 → _____

Think Tank

Gulls have 2 legs. Goats have 4 legs. How many legs altogether would 7 gulls and 5 goats have?

_____

Show your work in the tank. Explain your thinking.

_____

_____

Data Place

The box at right shows the birthdays of 5 friends. All were born in 2006.

Place and label each friend's birthday on the timeline. One is done for you. Then answer the questions.

Carly	December 3
Dave	June 10
Keith	May 25
Mara	January 9
Nanci	October 22

Mara

JAN   FEB   MAR   APR   MAY   JUN   JUL   AUG   SEP   OCT   NOV   DEC

1. Which friends' birthdays are closest? _____

2. Whose birthdays are in the fall? _____

3. Which friend is the oldest? _____ The youngest? _____

Puzzler

Many things come in groups. Our eyes, ears, legs, and hands come in 2s.

Fill in the chart with something that comes in each size group.

Hint: Think about nature, machines, sports, things you buy, and clothing.

3s	
4s	
5s	
6s	
7s	
8s	
9s	
10s	

Morning Jumpstarts: Math, Grade 3 © 2013 by Scholastic Teaching Resources

Name _____ Date _____

Number Place

Write any number that belongs *between*.

214 < _____ < 235   514 > _____ > 390

765 < _____ < 801   609 > _____ > 527

893 < _____ < 946   378 > _____ > 186

FAST Math

Add. Then multiply.

6 + 6 + 6 = _____   7 + 7 + 7 = _____

6 + 6 + 6 + 6 = _____   7 + 7 + 7 + 7 = _____

6 + 6 + 6 + 6 + 6 = _____   7 + 7 + 7 + 7 + 7 = _____

So, what is 6 × 6? _____   So, what is 6 × 7? _____

Think Tank

A shirt has 5 buttons down the front and 2 buttons on each sleeve. How many buttons are there in all on 3 shirts?

_____

Show your work in the tank. Explain your thinking.

Data Place

Make a bar graph with the library data.
Then answer the questions.

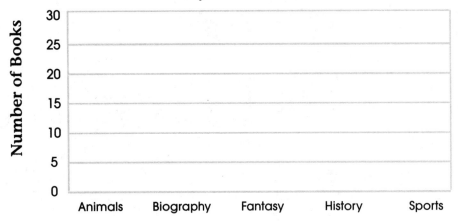

Library Books on Loan

Books on Loan

Animals 29

Biography 13

Fantasy 22

History 18

Sports 9

1. How many kinds of books are on loan? _____

2. How did you decide the heights of the bars? _____

Puzzler

Do you know the medical word for *sneezing*?

Use the clues below to solve the riddle.

— — — — — — — — — — — — —

The second, seventh, and ninth letters are *t*.

The eighth letter is *a*.

The third letter is *e*.

The tenth letter is *i*.

The eleventh letter is *o*.

The sixth letter is *u*.

The fourth letter is *r*.

The first letter is *s*.

The fifth and twelfth letters are *n*.

JUMPSTART 23

Name _____ Date _____

Number Place

• What number is 30 *more* than 362? _____

• What number is 50 *more* than 1234? _____

• What number is 20 *less* than 471? _____

• What number is 40 *less* than 700? _____

FAST Math

Find each product. Circle two products that are the same.

4 × 3 = _____   4 × 5 = _____   2 × 7 = _____

1 × 7 = _____   7 × 3 = _____   9 × 2 = _____

3 × 6 = _____   3 × 8 = _____   2 × 8 = _____

Think Tank

The temperature at noon was 72°F. Then strong cold winds blew in from the north. The temperature began to fall. By 4:00 P.M. it was 28° colder than it was at noon. What was the 4:00 P.M. temperature?

_____

Show your work in the tank. Explain your thinking. _____

_____

Morning Jumpstarts: Math, Grade 3 © 2013 by Scholastic Teaching Resources

Data Place

Students took a survey about sports gear they use the most.

Graph the data shown in the tally table. Then answer the questions.

Sports Gear Used Most

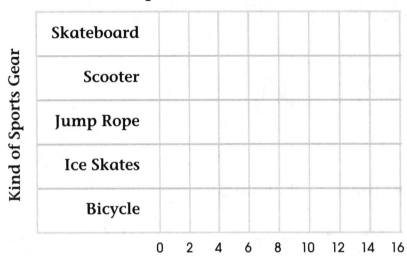

Sports Gear Used Most	
Bicycle	卌 卌 |||
Ice Skates	卌
Jump Rope	卌 卌	
Scooter	卌 ||||
Skateboard	卌 |||

1. Why might ice skates be used least often? _____

2. Which 2 items totaled 20 votes? _____

Puzzler

Each number has a different shape around it in the tic-tac-toe grid. For instance, ⌐ stands for 8. Do you see why?

Use this code to solve the problems.

1	2	3
4	5	6
7	8	9

1. ⌐ ⌐ ⌐ + ⌐ ⌐ ⌐ = _____

2. ⌐ ⌐ × ⌐ = _____

3. ⌐ ⌐ ⌐ − ⌐ ⌐ ⌐ = _____

4. ⌐ ⌐ ÷ ⌐ = _____

Morning Jumpstarts: Math, Grade 3 © 2013 by Scholastic Teaching Resources

JUMPSTART 24

Side A

Name _____ Date _____

Number Place

• What number is 200 *more* than 609? _____

• What number is 300 *more* than 5,231? _____

• What number is 300 *less* than 825? _____

• What number is 500 *less* than 2,674? _____

FAST Math

Find each product. Circle two products that are the same.

$5 \times 5 =$ _____ $4 \times 8 =$ _____ $4 \times 9 =$ _____

$6 \times 7 =$ _____ $6 \times 6 =$ _____ $8 \times 6 =$ _____

$3 \times 9 =$ _____ $7 \times 5 =$ _____ $7 \times 7 =$ _____

Think Tank

A floor is made with square tiles. Each tile is 1 foot long on a side. Look at the picture. What is the area of the floor in square feet?

_____

Show your work in the tank. Explain your thinking.

_____

_____

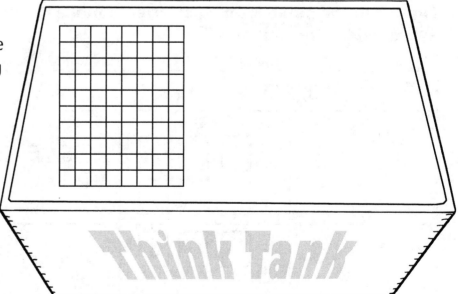

Morning Jumpstarts: Math, Grade 3 © 2013 by Scholastic Teaching Resources

55

Data Place

Kitty-Cat Castle is having a sale on some popular items.

Use the price list to answer the questions.

1. How much more is a bag of litter than a food dish?

   _____

2. Ray spent $5.63 on 2 items. What are they?

   _____

3. Gina buys 3 catnip toys. She pays with a $5 bill. How much change should she receive?

   _____

Kitty-Cat Castle Sale!

Item	Price
Bag of Litter	$3.79
Catnip Toy	$1.25
Flea Collar	$4.38
Food Dish	$2.40

Puzzler

Each problem is shown mostly in letters.
Above each problem are the rest of the numbers it needs.

**Figure out the number for each letter to make the problems work.
Two are done for you.**

0, 2, 3, 5		5, 6, 7, 8	
A L P + A L L L E 8	☐ ☐ ☐ + ☐ ☐ ☐ ☐ ☐ 8	S E E – M E A S O	☐ ☐ ☐ – ☐ ☐ ☐ ☐ 0

Morning Jumpstarts: Math, Grade 3 © 2013 by Scholastic Teaching Resources

Name _____ Date _____

Number Place

Order each set of numbers from *greatest* to *least*.

7,061   7,106   7,601   7,160   _____

5,859   5,985   5,589   5,958   _____

3,142   3,214   3,241   3,124   _____

FAST Math ➤

Find each product. Circle products in the same fact family.

$8 \times 8 =$ _____ $7 \times 8 =$ _____ $8 \times 9 =$ _____

$6 \times 9 =$ _____ $6 \times 7 =$ _____ $8 \times 7 =$ _____

$9 \times 7 =$ _____ $9 \times 6 =$ _____ $9 \times 9 =$ _____

💡 Think Tank

Leon makes a big L on grid paper. How many units are in the perimeter of his letter?

_____

Show your work in the tank. Explain your thinking.

_____

_____

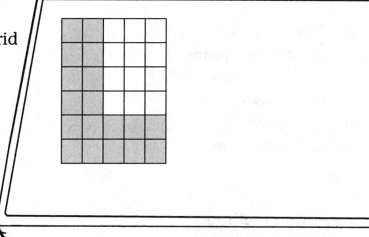

_____

Data Place

Give the number pair
where you find
each object.

1.  _____

2.  _____

3. _____

4.  _____

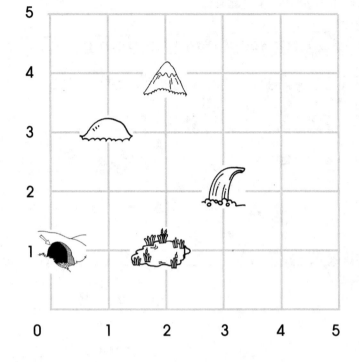

5. What do you see at (2, 1)? _____

Puzzler

Write the digits 2–8 *once* each in the
blank boxes of the magic square.
The sum of each row, column, and
diagonal must be 15. Two of the
digits are already in place.
Figure out where to place the
rest of them.

	9	
	1	

Explain your solution method. _____

_____

_____

_____

58

Morning Jumpstarts: Math, Grade 3 © 2013 by Scholastic Teaching Resources

Name _____ Date _____

Number Place

Order each set of numbers from *least* to *greatest*.

8,570 8,705 8,057 8,750 _____

6,932 6,293 6,923 6,392 _____

4,401 4,410 4,104 4,140 _____

FAST Math

Find each product. Circle the *greatest* product.

8 × 10 = _____   7 × 40 = _____   1 × 70 = _____

6 × 20 = _____   4 × 50 = _____   2 × 80 = _____

9 × 30 = _____   3 × 60 = _____   5 × 90 = _____

Think Tank

Gemma has 5 coins in her pocket. The coins add up to 61¢. What coins does she have?

Show your work in the tank. Explain your thinking.

_____

_____

_____

Data Place

A repair shop keeps extra computer keys in a drawer. How many of each kind do you see?

Count and tally them below.

Computer Keys

Key	Tally	Number
* 8		
K		
F5		
Alt		

How many computer keys in all? _____

Puzzler

Find the perimeter of the 4 on the grid.

_____ units

Find its area.

_____ square units

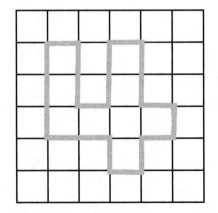

60

Name _____ Date _____

Number Place

Finish labeling the decimal number line.

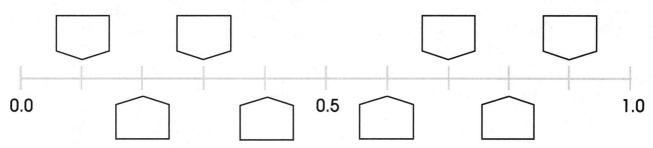

0.0   0.5   1.0

FAST Math

Find each product. Circle the *least* 4-digit product.

$2 \times 900 =$ _____ $6 \times 600 =$ _____ $8 \times 300 =$ _____

$1 \times 800 =$ _____ $5 \times 500 =$ _____ $7 \times 200 =$ _____

$3 \times 700 =$ _____ $4 \times 400 =$ _____ $9 \times 100 =$ _____

Think Tank

July is a month that always has 31 days. Look at the July calendar in the tank. Which days of the week appear 5 times that month?

_____

_____

_____

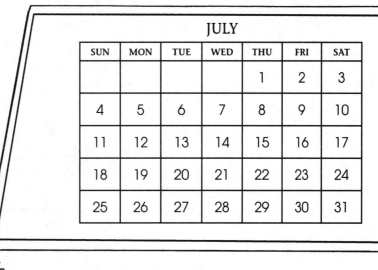

JULY

SUN	MON	TUE	WED	THU	FRI	SAT
				1	2	3
4	5	6	7	8	9	10
11	12	13	14	15	16	17
18	19	20	21	22	23	24
25	26	27	28	29	30	31

Think Tank

Data Place

Students at Lake School voted to name the new mascot—a brown female kitten.

Use the results of the vote to answer the questions.

Name	Votes
Cocoa	199
Maple	145
Rusty	201
Sienna	202
Toast	124

1. Close results led to a run-off election. The 2 lowest scoring names were out. Which names were those?

   _____

2. Everyone voted again. This time, 101 more people voted for Sienna than they did before. Rusty got 95 more votes than before. Cocoa got 73 more votes than before.

   What was the winning name? _____

   How many votes behind was the second place name? _____

Puzzler

Half of the design appears above a line of symmetry.
Shade the rest of the design. Keep it symmetrical.

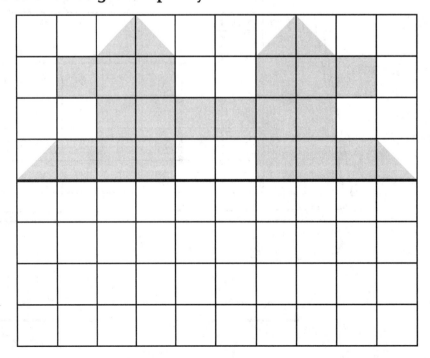

Name _____ Date _____

Number Place

Write each fraction as a decimal. Circle the decimal for *half*.

$\frac{1}{10}$ = _0.1_ $\frac{3}{10}$ = _____ $\frac{2}{10}$ = _____

$\frac{6}{10}$ = _____ $\frac{8}{10}$ = _____ $\frac{7}{10}$ = _____

$\frac{9}{10}$ = _____ $\frac{5}{10}$ = _____ $\frac{4}{10}$ = _____

FAST Math

Find each quotient. Circle the fact that is hardest for you.

9 ÷ 3 = _____   7 ÷ 1 = _____   18 ÷ 2 = _____

12 ÷ 2 = _____   15 ÷ 3 = _____   12 ÷ 3 = _____

18 ÷ 3 = _____   14 ÷ 2 = _____   9 ÷ 1 = _____

Think Tank

A snail falls into a hole 12 inches deep. Each day the snail climbs up 3 inches. But each night, it slides down 1 inch. Draw a picture in the tank to help you find out how many days the snail needs to get out of the hole.

_____

Data Place

Scouts raised money by selling boxes of cookies.
The table shows the top sellers.

Make a pictograph of the data.
Give it a title and a key.
Use ☐ to stand for 4 boxes.

Scout	Boxes Sold
Jenna	32
Brooke	40
Lucy	28
Eva	36

_____

Key: ☐ =

Puzzler

Use the fraction code to spell new words.
Write the letters in the order they appear in the clues.

The first $\frac{2}{3}$ of **pop.**

The second $\frac{1}{2}$ of **only.**

The first $\frac{1}{2}$ of **goat.**

The last $\frac{1}{4}$ of **rain.**

_____

The last $\frac{3}{5}$ of **extra.**

The first $\frac{2}{5}$ of **penny.**

The first $\frac{2}{3}$ of **zoo.**

The first $\frac{1}{2}$ of **idea.**

_____

Make up your own fraction code to spell your last name. Use another sheet of paper.

Morning Jumpstarts: Math, Grade 3 © 2013 by Scholastic Teaching Resources

Name _____ Date _____

Number Place
....

Write each decimal as a fraction. Circle the *greatest* decimal.

0.5 = $\frac{5}{10}$ 0.1 = _____   0.2 = _____

0.3 = _____   0.6 = _____   0.9 = _____

0.8 = _____   0.4 = _____   0.7 = _____

FAST Math ▶

Find each quotient. Circle the fact that is hardest for you.

4 ÷ 4 = _____   8 ÷ 4 = _____   32 ÷ 4 = _____

30 ÷ 5 = _____   28 ÷ 4 = _____   16 ÷ 4 = _____

20 ÷ 5 = _____   40 ÷ 5 = _____   5 ÷ 5 = _____

💡 Think Tank
....

Kit's class has 27 students. Kit is ninth in line for gym. How many students are ahead of him?

_____

Behind him?

_____

Show your work in the tank.

Data Place

Use the graph to answer the questions about people's least favorite veggie.

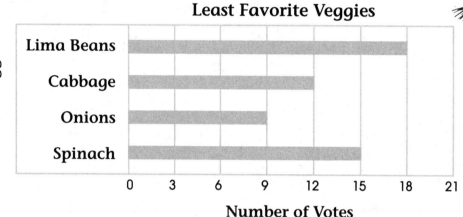

Least Favorite Veggies

Kind of Veggie

- Lima Beans
- Cabbage
- Onions
- Spinach

0   3   6   9   12   15   18   21

Number of Votes

1. Which veggies do 12 or fewer people dislike? _____

2. Which veggie do people dislike twice as much as onions? _____

Puzzler

Draw a picture to help you solve this money puzzle.

Wyatt put 8 pennies in a row on his desk.
Then he swapped every 2nd penny for a dime.
Next, he swapped every 3rd coin for a nickel.
Finally, he swapped every 4th coin for a quarter.

1. How much money is on the desk now? _____

2. How much more is it than Wyatt started with? _____

66

Name _____ Date _____

Number Place

Compare. Write < or >.

0.4 ◯ 0.3   0.7 ◯ 0.2   0.1 ◯ 0.4

0.5 ◯ 0.8   0.6 ◯ 0.9   0.8 ◯ 0.7

FAST Math

Find each quotient. Circle the fact that is hardest for you.

24 ÷ 6 = _____   42 ÷ 7 = _____   36 ÷ 6 = _____

35 ÷ 7 = _____   28 ÷ 7 = _____   49 ÷ 7 = _____

48 ÷ 6 = _____   54 ÷ 6 = _____   63 ÷ 7 = _____

Think Tank

A basketball goal is worth 2 points. Karen scored 24 points in a game. Bree scored half as many points in that game. How many goals did Karen and Bree make in all?

_____

Show your work in the tank. Explain your thinking.

_____

_____

Morning Jumpstarts: Math, Grade 3 © 2013 by Scholastic Teaching Resources

Data Place

Zoe counted the sit-ups she did each day.

Monday	80
Tuesday	70
Wednesday	100
Thursday	50
Friday	90

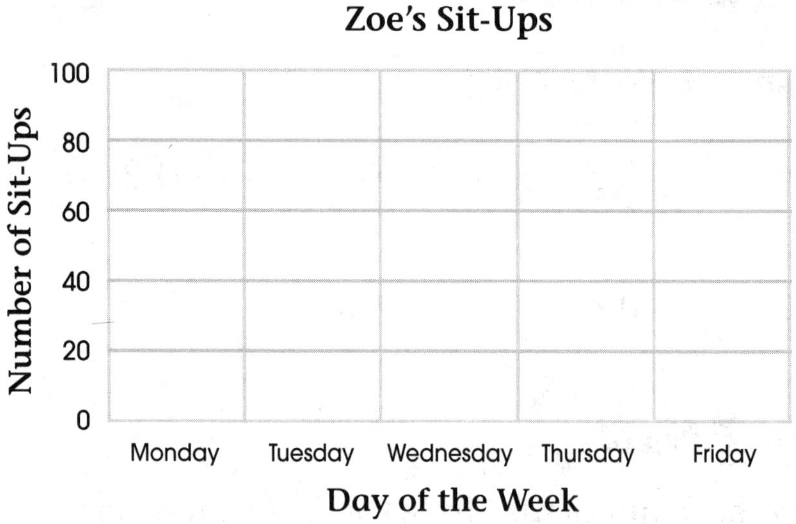
Zoe's Sit-Ups
Number of Sit-Ups
100
80
60
40
20
0
Monday
Tuesday
Wednesday
Thursday
Friday
Day of the Week

Make a bar graph to show the sit-ups Zoe did.

Find the difference between the most and least sit-ups Zoe did that week.

____

Puzzler

This coordinate grid has 20 letters on it.

Write the ordered pairs to spell a word for each clue.

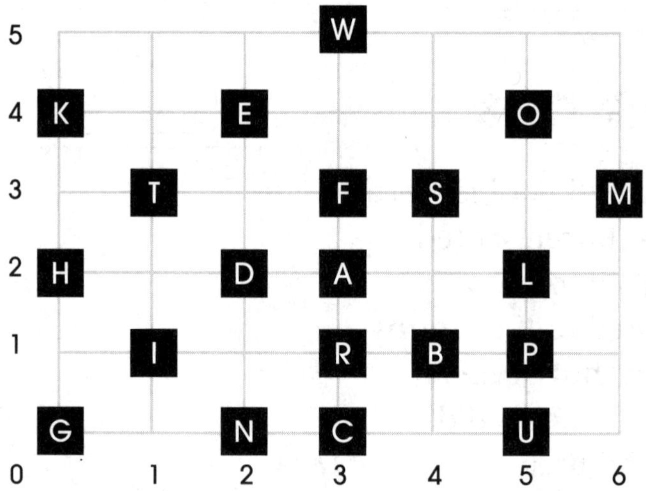
W
5
4
K
E
O
3
T
F
S
M
2
H
D
A
L
1
I
R
B
P
G
N
C
U
0
1
2
3
4
5
6

A color: ______________________________

A tool: ______________________________

A cartoon character: ______________________________

A food: ______________________________

Morning Jumpstarts: Math, Grade 3 © 2013 by Scholastic Teaching Resources

Name _____ Date _____

Number Place

Order the decimals from *least* to *greatest*.

0.6 0.2 0.9 0.4   _____

0.3 0.7 0.8 0.1   _____

Order the decimals from *greatest* to *least*.

0.1 0.8 0.4 0.6   _____

0.7 0.3 0.5 0.9   _____

FAST Math

Find each quotient. Circle the fact that is hardest for you.

$18 \div 9 =$ _____ $81 \div 9 =$ _____ $64 \div 8 =$ _____

$32 \div 8 =$ _____ $27 \div 9 =$ _____ $72 \div 9 =$ _____

$48 \div 8 =$ _____ $40 \div 8 =$ _____ $63 \div 9 =$ _____

Think Tank

D'nae walked 4 blocks to the bus stop. She then rode the bus 21 blocks to the dentist. She went home the same way. How many blocks did D'nae travel in all?

_____

Show your work in the tank. Explain your thinking.

Data Place

Use the pictograph to answer the questions.

Stamps Sold Yesterday

Lady Liberty	☐ ☐ ☐ ☐ ☐ ☐ ☐ ☐ ☐ ☐ ☐ ☐
Lincoln	☐ ☐ ☐ ☐ ☐ ☐ ☐
Eagle	☐ ☐ ☐ ☐ ☐ ☐ ☐ ☐ ☐
Flag	☐ ☐ ☐ ☐ ☐ ☐ ☐ ☐ ☐

Key: ☐ = 10 stamps

1. How many different designs were sold? _____

2. Which stamp sold the least? _____

   How many stamps of that kind were sold? _____

3. Which 2 designs sold a total of 175 stamps? _____

4. If 1 stamp costs 45¢, how much do 10 stamps cost? _____

Puzzler

Write the numbers 100, 200, 300, 400,
and 500 *once* each in the 5 boxes.
Make the sum of the 3 numbers
in each direction total 1,000.
Explain how you solved the problem.

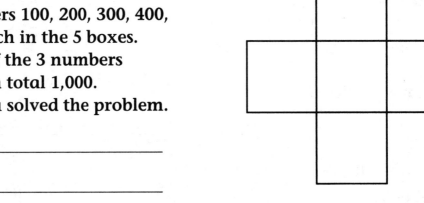

_____

_____

_____

Morning Jumpstarts: Math, Grade 3 © 2013 by Scholastic Teaching Resources

Name _____ Date _____

Number Place

Finish labeling the decimal number line.

0.46   0.50   0.60

___ ___ ___ ___   ___ ___ ___ ___ ___ ___ ___ ___

FAST Math

Find each product as quickly as you can.

8 × 9 = _____   5 × 6 = _____   7 × 7 = _____

7 × 8 = _____   4 × 0 = _____   4 × 7 = _____

6 × 7 = _____   1 × 3 = _____   8 × 6 = _____

Think Tank

Tonya made a pecan pie. She cut it into 8 equal pieces. She served $\frac{3}{8}$ for dessert. She packed $\frac{3}{8}$ of the pie for lunches the next day. What fraction of the pie is still left?

_____

Draw your solution in the tank.

Data Place

Finish the table about the number of letters in the last names of third graders. Then answer the questions.

Letters in Last Names of Third Graders

Range	Tallies	Number
1–3	卌 I	
4–6		38
7–9	卌 卌 卌 卌 卌 卌 IIII	
10–12	卌 卌 卌 II	
13 or more		7

1. Which range includes Mr. Gold's name? _____

2. Which range would include your last name? _____

3. Which range has twice as many names as 10–12? _____

Puzzler

Color the design. Use the key.

KEY	
If the fraction is	Color the space
$= \frac{1}{2}$	blue
$= 1$	red
$< \frac{1}{2}$	yellow

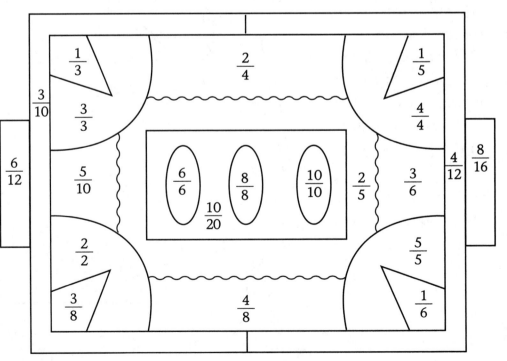

Morning Jumpstarts: Math, Grade 3 © 2013 by Scholastic Teaching Resources

Name _____ Date _____

Number Place

Write each fraction as a decimal. Circle the decimal for *half*.

$\frac{45}{100}$ = 0.45 $\frac{30}{100}$ = _____ $\frac{72}{100}$ = _____

$\frac{63}{100}$ = _____ $\frac{81}{100}$ = _____ $\frac{94}{100}$ = _____

$\frac{29}{100}$ = _____ $\frac{5}{100}$ = _____ $\frac{50}{100}$ = _____

FAST Math

Find each quotient as quickly as you can.

$27 \div 3$ = _____ $56 \div 7$ = _____ $24 \div 4$ = _____

$63 \div 9$ = _____ $45 \div 5$ = _____ $0 \div 2$ = _____

$42 \div 6$ = _____ $48 \div 8$ = _____ $63 \div 7$ = _____

Think Tank

Sasha is a tour guide at History Village. Each tour she gives lasts for $1\frac{1}{4}$ hours.

How long do 3 tours take?

_____

Show your work in the tank.

Data Place

The 5 Great Lakes are so big they can be seen from space!

Make a bar graph to compare their lengths. Use the data in the table. Give the graph a title.

The Great Lakes	Length in Miles
Huron	206
Ontario	193
Michigan	307
Erie	241
Superior	350

_____

Name of Lake	
Huron	
Ontario	
Michigan	
Erie	
Superior	

0 25 50 75 100 125 150 175 200 225 250 275 300 325 350 375

Number of Miles

Write the names of the Great Lakes in length order from longest to shortest.

_____

_____

Puzzler

Use 13 toothpicks to make a cat walking to the right, as shown. Now move only 2 toothpicks to make the cat walk to the left.

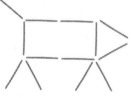

Explain how you solved this puzzle.

_____

_____

74

Morning Jumpstarts: Math, Grade 3 © 2013 by Scholastic Teaching Resources

Name _____ Date _____

Number Place

Write each decimal as a fraction. Circle the *least* decimal.

0.38 = $\frac{38}{100}$ 0.03 = _____   0.26 = _____

0.75 = _____   0.61 = _____   0.98 = _____

0.40 = _____   0.52 = _____   0.86 = _____

FAST Math

Write each fact family.

8, 5, 13	7, 8, 56
____ + ____ = ____	____ × ____ = ____
____ + ____ = ____	____ × ____ = ____
____ − ____ = ____	____ ÷ ____ = ____
____ − ____ = ____	____ ÷ ____ = ____

Think Tank

A soup recipe needs 1.3 kilograms of cabbage, 0.2 kilograms of onions, and 0.4 kilograms of carrots. How many kilograms of vegetables go into the soup?

_____

Show your work in the tank.

Data Place

The table shows how many miles inside Texas its 5 longest rivers flow.

River	Miles in Texas
Brazos	846
Colorado	600
Red	680
Rio Grande	1,250
Trinity	550

Use the data in the table to answer the questions.

1. Which 2 Texas rivers are only 50 miles apart in length?

   _____

   _____

2. How much longer is the longest river than the shortest one? _____

3. Which river flows about 700 miles in Texas? _____

Puzzler

Find a path through every white box (*only once*) without lifting your pencil.

Start and end at the rocket. You may not go through the gray boxes.

Hint: Try with your finger first.

Morning Jumpstarts: Math, Grade 3 © 2013 by Scholastic Teaching Resources

Name _____ Date _____

Number Place

Compare. Write <, >, or =.

0.14 ◯ 0.41   0.65 ◯ 0.6   0.33 ◯ 0.4

0.57 ◯ 0.50   0.90 ◯ 0.9   0.6 ◯ 0.08

FAST Math ▶

Multiply. Circle the factors that have the same product.

$2 \times 2 \times 2 =$ _____ $3 \times 4 \times 2 =$ _____ $6 \times 4 \times 2 =$ _____

$3 \times 3 \times 3 =$ _____ $7 \times 5 \times 1 =$ _____ $9 \times 7 \times 0 =$ _____

$1 \times 2 \times 7 =$ _____ $5 \times 0 \times 8 =$ _____ $6 \times 2 \times 5 =$ _____

💡 Think Tank

Lizzy's 3-person team won the relay race on Field Day. Each runner's separate time is shown below. What was the total time for the winning team?

_____

Winning Team	
Lizzy	1.15 minutes
Zora	1.33 minutes
Shen	1.09 minutes

Show your work in the tank.

Data Place

Mrs. Chen gives a 15-word spelling test every Friday. The line plot shows students' scores on the most recent test.

Use the line plot to answer the questions below.

Words Spelled Correctly

		X	
	X	X	
	X	X	X
	X	X	X
X	X	X	X
X	X	X	X
12 Words	**13 Words**	**14 Words**	**15 Words**

1. How many students took the test?

   _____

2. How many students spelled all 15 words correctly? _____

3. How many students missed 1 word? _____

4. How many students missed 3 words? _____

5. Describe something about the test scores you *cannot* know from the line plot.

   _____

Puzzler

All insects have 6 legs. All spiders have 8 legs. Some insects and spiders went to a garden dance. There were 48 dancing legs.

Figure out how many insects and how many spiders were at the dance.

Hint: Try guess-and-check.

_____ insects and _____ spiders.

Name _____ Date _____

Number Place

Order the decimals from *least* to *greatest*.

0.12	0.49	0.35	_____
0.63	0.2	0.49	_____
0.4	0.43	0.38	_____
0.75	0.7	0.06	_____

FAST Math ➤

Write the time to the minute. **X** a time when school may end.

_____ _____ _____ _____

💡 Think Tank

Traci makes a big T on grid paper. What is the area of her letter in square units?

_____

Show your work in the tank. Explain your thinking.

_____

_____

_____

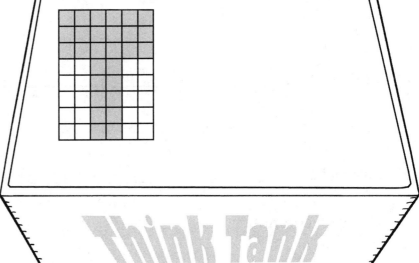

Data Place

Use the data in the calendar to answer the questions.

APRIL

SUN	MON	TUE	WED	THU	FRI	SAT
			1	2	3	4
5	6	7	8	9	10	11
12	13	14	15	16	17	18
19	20	21	22	23	24	25
26	27	28	29	30		

1. Two dates in a row have a sum of 35. What are the dates?

   _____

2. Two dates in a row have a product of 90. What are the dates?

   _____

3. There is a field trip on the last Tuesday of the month. What is its date? _____

4. On what day will May 8th fall? _____

Puzzler

Follow these steps for a surprising age trick.

1. Double your age. _____

2. Add 5. _____

3. Multiply by 5. _____

4. Add the number of people in your family. _____

5. Subtract 25. _____

6. What do you notice in the answer? _____

Morning Jumpstarts: Math, Grade 3 © 2013 by Scholastic Teaching Resources

Name _____ Date _____

Number Place

Write the decimal from the balloon that fits each clue.

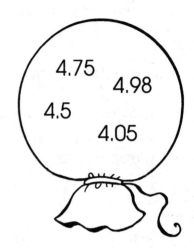

_____ is much nearer to 4 than to 5.

_____ is halfway between 4 and 5.

_____ is the same as $4\frac{3}{4}$.

_____ is a little less than 5.

Balloon: 4.75 4.98 4.5 4.05

FAST Math ▶

Count the money. Write how much with $ and .

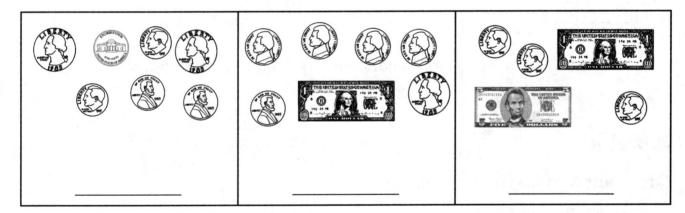

_____   _____   _____

💡 Think Tank

Harriet Tubman was a brave African-American hero. She risked her life helping slaves escape to freedom. She was born in 1822, and died in 1913. How old did Tubman live to be?

_____

Show your work in the tank.

Data Place

All the students at Grady School took a survey about parades. The table shows what they liked best.

Parade Parts	Votes
Balloons	109
Bands	197
Costumes	88
Floats	125

Use the data to answer the questions.

1. Find the difference in votes between the most popular and least popular parade parts.

   _____

2. Which 2 parade parts got as many votes as the most popular part? Explain your answer.

   _____

3. How many more votes would balloons need to tie for 2nd place? _____

Puzzler

Skip count by 4s to connect the dots.

Hint: There are 7 numbers not used.

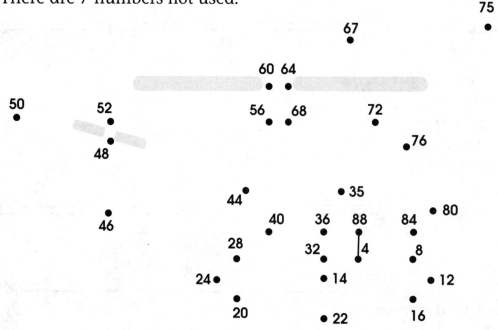

Morning Jumpstarts: Math, Grade 3 © 2013 by Scholastic Teaching Resources

Name _____ Date _____

Number Place

Write each in decimal form.

• seven tenths   _____

• three and five tenths   _____

• forty-five hundredths   _____

• nine and eleven hundredths   _____

FAST Math

Add or subtract. Circle the answer nearest to $8.

$5.27	$5.49	$7.03	$8.00	$3.60	$6.07
+ 3.83	− 2.66	+ 1.89	− 5.62	+ 4.56	− 2.78
_____	_____	_____	_____	_____	_____

Think Tank

Kobuk Valley National Park is in Alaska. It opened in 1982, and got 3,775 visitors. In 1987, only 230 visitors came. How many more visitors saw Kobuk Valley in 1982 than in 1987?

_____

Show your work in the tank.

Morning Jumpstarts: Math, Grade 3 © 2013 by Scholastic Teaching Resources

Data Place

The Four-Plex is showing the movies listed in the schedule.

Use the data to answer the questions.

MOVIE	Starts	Ends
Action Alley	1:40	3:25
Space Racers	1:25	3:10
Time Travel	2:00	3:40
Zebra Force	2:10	3:45

1. Which movie starts the earliest?

   _____

2. Which is the shortest movie? _____

3. Which 2 movies last the same number of minutes? _____

   _____

4. Kate's dad will drop her off at 1:50. Which movie do you think she will see?

   Explain. _____

Puzzler

Fill in this design using 4 different colors. You can repeat colors—but not where sections touch.

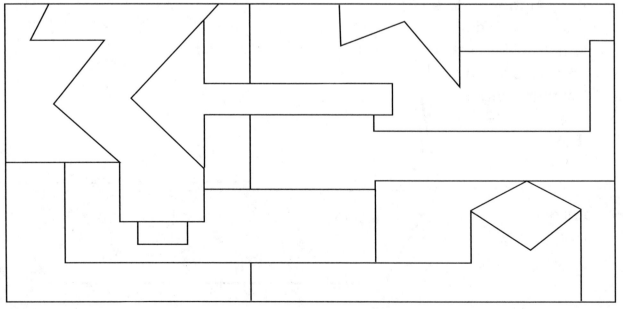

Morning Jumpstarts: Math, Grade 3 © 2013 by Scholastic Teaching Resources

Name _____ Date _____

Number Place

Write each decimal in word form.

0.8 _____   0.42 _____

1.1 _____   3.59 _____

FAST Math ➤

Shade each fractional part. Circle the fraction nearest to one whole.

$\frac{1}{3}$	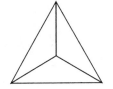	$\frac{3}{5}$	
$\frac{5}{6}$	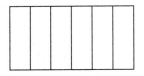	$\frac{1}{2}$	

💡 Think Tank

Most adult dogs have 42 teeth. How many teeth would 4 adult dogs have?

_____

Show your work in the tank. Explain your thinking.

_____

_____

_____

Data Place

Use the garden shop price list to answer the questions.

Fresh Vegetables!

Plant	Price
Bean	$2.99
Corn	$1.70
Celery	$2.20
Tomato	$3.33

1. Four bean plants would cost about

   $ _____ .

2. How many corn plants could you buy with $10?

   _____

3. Which costs more: 3 celery plants or 2 tomato plants?

   _____

   How much more? _____

Puzzler

Solve the clock-face riddles.
Write 2 times when the clock hands would:

1. form a square corner: _____ and _____

2. form a straight line: _____ and _____

3. form mirror images: _____ and _____

4. overlap: _____ and _____

Hint: Use the blank clocks to help you figure out the answers.

Morning Jumpstarts: Math, Grade 3 © 2013 by Scholastic Teaching Resources

Name _____ Date _____

Number Place

Write each decimal in expanded form.

0.38 _____

1.4 _____

2.06 _____

7.77 _____

FAST Math

Write a fraction for the gray part(s). Circle the figure that shows *half*.

_____ _____ _____ _____

💡 Think Tank

Granddad is 64 years old. Mother is half Granddad's age. Muffy, the cat, is half Mother's age. How old is Muffy?

_____

Show your work in the tank. Explain your thinking.

_____

Data Place

Use the frequency table to count and
tally every vowel in the tongue twister.

Vowel	Tally	Number
a		
e		
i		
o		
u		

Bettie Butler
bought
a bit of bitter
butter.

How would the table change if *Bettie* spelled her name *Betty*? Explain.

_____

_____

Puzzler

Color the design.
Use the key.

KEY	
If the decimal is	Color the space
> 1.0	blue
= 0.5	purple
< 0.5	green

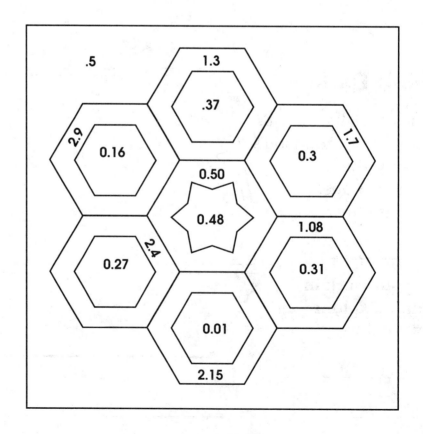

JUMPSTART 41

Side A

Name _____ Date _____

Number Place
. . . .

Circle the greater amount.

$.55 or 5 dimes   5 nickels or $.20

$1.07 or 11 dimes   5 quarters or $1.20

$.80 or 3 quarters   4 quarters or $1.04

FAST Math ➤

Finish labeling the fraction number line.

$$\frac{0}{8} \qquad\qquad \frac{3}{8} \qquad\qquad\qquad\qquad \frac{8}{8}$$

Think Tank
. . . .

Pia and Lu collect toy ducks.
Together they have 51 of
them! Lu has 7 more toy
ducks than Pia has. How
many toy ducks does
Lu have?

_____

How many does Pia have?

_____

Show your work in the tank.
Explain your thinking.

_____

_____

Morning Jumpstarts: Math, Grade 3 © 2013 by Scholastic Teaching Resources

Data Place

Complete a bar graph to
show the attendance at 4
performances of an ice show.
Give the graph a title, labels,
and horizontal bars. Fill in the
numbers at the bottom.

Day	Attendance
Thursday	228
Friday	345
Saturday	386
Sunday	297

```
0      50     100    ____    200    ____    300    350    ____
```

Puzzler

Circle 5 pairs of addends that
total 100. Pairs must touch
horizontally ⟷ or vertically ↕ .

82	59	52	48
18	41	73	96
26	74	37	4

Morning Jumpstarts: Math, Grade 3 © 2013 by Scholastic Teaching Resources

Name _____   Date _____

Number Place

Write any 2 decimal numbers that belong *between*.
Write 1 decimal in tenths and the other in hundredths.

0 < _____ < _____ < 1   7 < _____ < _____ < 8

2 < _____ < _____ < 3   10 < _____ < _____ < 11

FAST Math ▶

Circle all fractions equivalent to *half*.

$\frac{5}{5}$	$\frac{2}{4}$	$\frac{3}{4}$	$\frac{5}{10}$	$\frac{6}{8}$	$\frac{3}{6}$
$\frac{4}{8}$	$\frac{9}{10}$	$\frac{6}{12}$	$\frac{2}{1}$	$\frac{1}{3}$	$\frac{10}{20}$

What fraction of fractions in the box is *not* equivalent to half? _____

💡 Think Tank

A jet can carry 103 passengers. How many passengers in all could travel on 5 full flights?

_____

Use mental math to solve.

Use the tank if you need to.

Morning Jumpstarts: Math, Grade 3 © 2013 by Scholastic Teaching Resources

Data Place

Skip-count by 4s to 40. _____

_____

Skip-count by 6s to 60. _____

_____

Now put each number in the Venn diagram.

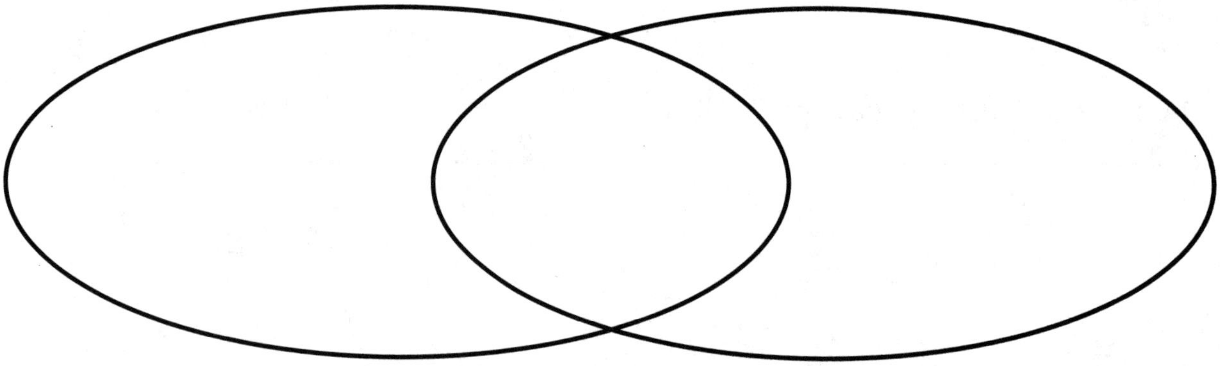

Multiples of 4   Both   Multiples of 6

Puzzler

Solve each number riddle.

1. Two numbers have a sum of 15. They have a product of 56.

   What are the numbers? _____ and _____

2. Two numbers have a difference of 5. They have a quotient of 2.

   What are the numbers? _____ and _____

3. Two numbers have a product of 40. They have a sum of 14.

   What are the numbers? _____ and _____

4. Two numbers have a difference of 0. They have a product of 81.

   What are the numbers? _____ and _____

Name _____ Date _____

Number Place

Use the numbers on the cards to form:

6	7
9	2

• the *greatest* number. _____

• the *least* number. _____

• the *greatest even* number. _____

• the *greatest odd* number. _____

FAST Math

Write the missing numbers to make each fraction equal 1.

 $\dfrac{\square}{5}$ $\dfrac{\square}{8}$ $\dfrac{\square}{2}$ $\dfrac{\square}{6}$ $\dfrac{\square}{10}$ $\dfrac{\square}{3}$

 $\dfrac{4}{\square}$ $\dfrac{1}{\square}$ $\dfrac{7}{\square}$ $\dfrac{9}{\square}$ $\dfrac{12}{\square}$ $\dfrac{16}{\square}$

Think Tank

A diner keeps 60 mugs on 3 shelves. Each shelf holds the same number of mugs. How many mugs go on each shelf?

_____

Use mental math to solve.

Use the tank if you need to.

Data Place

Use the circle graph to answer the
questions about people's favorite juice.

Favorite Juice

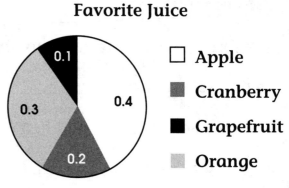

□ Apple
■ Cranberry (gray)
■ Grapefruit
■ Orange (light gray)

1. Which juice flavor got $\frac{3}{10}$ of the votes?

   _____

2. What fraction of the votes
   went for grapefruit juice?

   _____

3. Which flavor is twice as popular as cranberry? _____

4. If 100 people voted, how many chose apple juice? _____

Puzzler

Write a letter from the code to make each number sentence true.

A = 1	B = 2	C = 3	D = 4	E = 5	F = 6	G = 7
H = 8	I = 9	J = 10	K = 11	L = 12	M = 13	N = 14
O = 15	P = 16	Q = 17	R = 18	S = 19	T = 20	U = 21
V = 22	W = 23	X = 24	Y = 25	Z = 26		

1. $D \times$ _____ $= X$

2. $V \div K =$ _____

3. $Y -$ _____ $= G$

4. $J +$ _____ $= W$

5. _____ $- N = L$

6. $U \div$ _____ $= C$

7. $F \times$ _____ $= R$

8. $H + B +$ _____ $= U$

Morning Jumpstarts: Math, Grade 3 © 2013 by Scholastic Teaching Resources

Name _____ Date _____

Number Place

Write <, =, or >.

1,357 ◯ 1,375   88.8 ◯ 88   1.5 ◯ 1.50

6.02 ◯ 6.2   2,405 ◯ 2,450   2.9 ◯ 2.89

FAST Math

Write a mixed number for each picture.

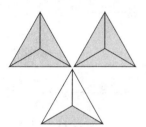 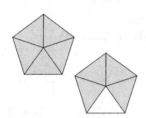 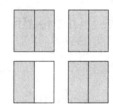 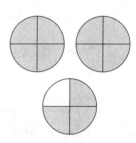

_____ _____ _____ _____

Think Tank

A subway car can fit up to 187 riders. Some sit, but most stand. Estimate about how many could ride on a subway train that has 8 cars.

_____

Show your work in the tank. Explain your estimate.

_____

_____

Morning Jumpstarts: Math, Grade 3 © 2013 by Scholastic Teaching Resources

Data Place

Gracie the dog has her own doggy calendar. The box shows 5 important dates next year.

Place and label each important date on the timeline. One is done for you. Then answer the questions.

Adoption Day	Apr 12
Birthday	Feb 10
Dog Park Party..........	Oct 17
National Dog Day	Aug 26
Vet Check-Up	Jun 4

Birthday

_____   _____   _____

JAN   FEB   MAR   APR   MAY   JUN   JUL   AUG   SEP   OCT   NOV   DEC

_____   _____

1. Which events happen in the first half of a month? _____

_____

2. About how much time is between Gracie's birthday and her adoption day?

_____

3. Which event happens in summer? _____

Puzzler

Each problem is shown in letters. Above each problem are the rest of the numbers it needs.

Figure out the number for each letter to make the problems work. One number is done for you.

1, 6, 7, 9		3, 9	
M E × 4 ——— U S	☐ ☐ × ☐ ——— ☐ ☐	Z Z Z Z) A A A	☐ ☐ ☐ ☐) ☐ ☐ ☐

Morning Jumpstarts: Math, Grade 3 © 2013 by Scholastic Teaching Resources

Name _____ Date _____

Number Place

Write the correct number from the box.
One number is *not* used.

| 23,689 | 30,868 | 48,732 |
| 70,320 | 97,536 | |

• It has as many ones as hundreds. _____

• Its digits are in order, from *least* to *greatest*. _____

• It has 8 thousands. _____

• The sum of its digits is 12. _____

FAST Math

Write the equivalent measurement.

2 cups = 1 _____

1 quart = _____ cups

2 pints = _____ quart

4 quarts = 1 _____

Cup   Pint   Quart   Gallon

Think Tank

An album has 10 pages.
$\frac{3}{10}$ of the album has photos.
$\frac{6}{10}$ has drawings. $\frac{1}{10}$ of
the album is blank.

What fraction of the
album has photos
and drawings? _____

Show your work
in the tank.

Think Tank

Jumpstart 45

Data Place

The table below shows results of a survey on best places to swim. But some of the table is blank.

Use the clues to fill in the table.

- Seven people choose ocean swimming.
- Most people prefer pool swimming.
- Twice as many people prefer a lake to a creek.

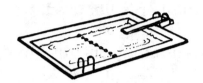

Place to Swim	Tally	Number
	‖‖‖ ‖‖‖	
		18
	‖‖‖ ‖‖‖ ‖‖‖ ‖‖‖ ‖‖‖	

Puzzler

Use logic to figure out what a _gloink_ is. Then solve.

Each of these is a _gloink_.				
None of these is a _gloink_.				

Circle all the _gloinks_.

1.	2.	3.	4.

What is the rule for a _gloink_?_____

_____

Name _____ Date _____

Number Place

Round each money amount to the nearest dime and dollar.

Amount	Nearest Dime	Nearest Dollar
$7.43		
$1.25		
$6.89		
$4.96		

FAST Math

Which measurement makes the most sense? Write *inches*, *feet*, *yards*, or *miles*.

Tim's best football pass was 27 _____ .

Mom drove 45 _____ to visit Grandpa.

A school bus is 36 _____ long.

A table lamp is 18 _____ tall.

Think Tank

Dad brought home a long loaf of bread. He cut it into eighths. The family ate $\frac{5}{8}$ of the bread with dinner. What fraction of the bread was left?

_____

Show your work in the tank.

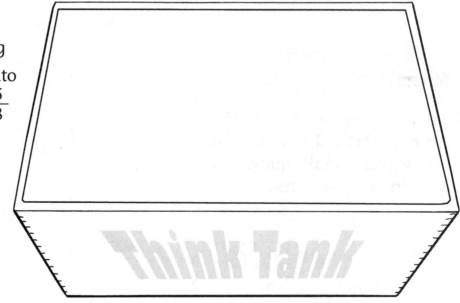

99

Data Place

Toss 2 number cubes 40 times. Make an X for each sum in the line plot below. You should have 40 Xs when you are done.

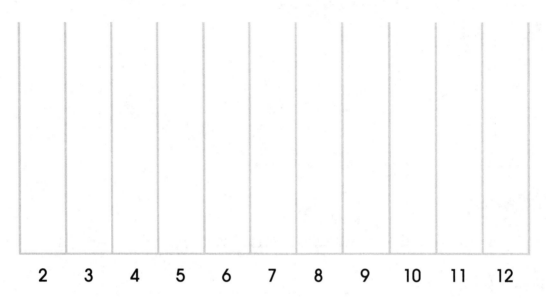

| 2 | 3 | 4 | 5 | 6 | 7 | 8 | 9 | 10 | 11 | 12 |

What interesting things do you see in the data?

_____

_____

_____

Puzzler

Solve the number puzzle. Use only the numbers 1, 2, 3, and 4 *once* inside every small square, and *once* in every row and column.

		4	
4	3		2
		2	1
1	2		

Name _____ Date _____

Number Place

Copy the correct number from the box.

- It has 4 hundredths. _____

- It has 4 tens. _____

- It has 4 tenths. _____

- It has 4 ones. _____

- It has 4 hundreds. _____

| 740.26 |
| 785.64 |
| 623.45 |
| 604.78 |
| 435.09 |

FAST Math

Use a ruler. Measure and label the gray lines to the nearest centimeter.

| 1. ⊢——⊣ _____ cm | 3. ⊢—————————⊣ _____ cm |
| 2. ⊢————⊣ _____ cm | 4. ⊢—⊣ _____ cm |

Think Tank

A library got a total of 87 new books and magazines. There were 21 more books than magazines. How many of each kind arrived?

_____ books

_____ magazines

Show your work in the tank.

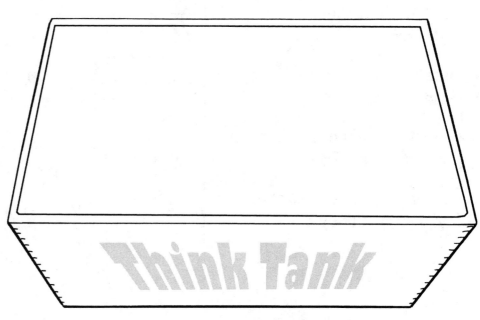

JUMPSTART 47

Side B

Data Place

Check out today's morning menu at Breakfast Bill's.

Breakfast Menu	
Oh-la-la Oatmeal	$1.75
Pecan Pancakes	$3.25
Tortillas & Eggs	$2.88
Fruit & Yogurt	$2.46
Muffins	$1.20
All Drinks	$1.00

Use the menu to answer the questions.

1. Dad gets 5 muffins and 5 drinks. He pays with $15. How much change should he get back? _____

2. Order breakfast and a drink. What will you have? _____

_____

How much will it cost? _____

3. You have $10. Can you afford 3 orders of pecan pancakes? Explain.

_____

Puzzler

Color the numbers in the grid.

- Use *red* when a number divides evenly by 3.

- Use *blue* when a number divides evenly by 4.

- Use *green* when a number divides evenly by 5.

5	14	59	11	23	53	21
46	25	7	37	26	5	47
31	13	6	4	3	2	17
26	43	8	32	16	34	19
7	49	18	28	9	29	61
34	35	19	41	7	50	23
27	1	22	13	38	2	10

102

Name _____ Date _____

Number Place

Solve the riddle about a 4-digit number that rounds to 4,000.

• All my digits are odd *and* different.

• I have 3 times as many thousands as ones.

• I have 3 times as many hundreds as thousands.

• I have no 7s.

The number is _____

FAST Math ▶

Multiply. Circle the product that rounds to 200.

32	41	22	304	110	21
× 3	× 2	× 4	× 2	× 7	× 8
———	———	———	———	———	———

💡 Think Tank

There are 12 months in 1 full year. A month can have 28, 29, 30, or 31 days in it. Zamir is 9 years old today. How many months old is he?

_____

Show your work in the tank.

Data Place

The table shows miles between some Florida cities. Go *across a row* for 1 city. Go *down a column* for another. The number where they meet is how many miles apart they are.

	Miami	Orlando	Tampa
Fort Myers	152	171	130
Key West	162	229	255
Sarasota	225	132	60

Use the data to answer the questions.

1. Which city is farthest from Miami? _____

2. Which 2 cities are 255 miles apart? _____

3. Which cities are nearest each other? _____

4. Fort Myers is _____ miles nearer to Miami than Key West is.

Puzzler

Shade a picture in each hundredths grid.
Draw anything you like—but make its area match the decimal.

0.34

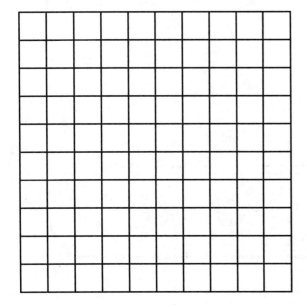

0.72

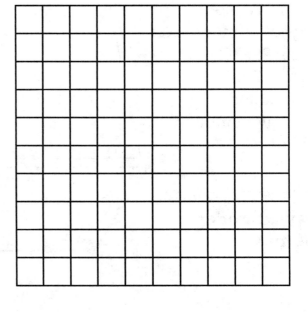

Name _____　Date _____

Number Place

Round each number to the nearest hundred and thousand.

Number	Nearest 100	Nearest 1,000
4,307		
9,153		
6,745		
8,068		

FAST Math

Divide. Circle the quotient that is *odd*.

$2\overline{)48}$　　$3\overline{)39}$　　$4\overline{)88}$　　$3\overline{)690}$　　$5\overline{)500}$　　$2\overline{)624}$

Think Tank

Look at the picture in the tank. Polly put together this solid figure out of snap cubes. How many cubes did she use to build it?

_____

Explain your thinking.

_____

_____

Data Place

The timetable shows 5 stops on the Oak Lane morning bus line.

Use the data to answer the questions.

From Oak Lane to:	Leaves	Trip Length
Ames Ave.	8:15	20 min.
Bank St.	8:40	15 min.
City Hall	9:05	10 min.
Drake Rd.	9:10	$\frac{1}{2}$ hour
Ellis Hospital	9:20	25 min.

1. What time would you get to Bank Street? _____

2. Nora took the City Hall bus, which got stuck in traffic for 15 minutes. What time did she get to City Hall? _____

3. The Ellis Hospital bus left 10 minutes late. What time did it get to Ellis Hospital? _____

4. Todd's bus made it to its stop exactly on time at 9:40. Which bus did he take?

_____

Puzzler

Rearrange the 7 toothpicks to form 3 equal triangles. Draw your solution in the box.

Morning Jumpstarts: Math, Grade 3 © 2013 by Scholastic Teaching Resources

Name _____ Date _____

Number Place

Use the number cards and decimal point to write a decimal that

8	0
3	•

• is a whole number. _____

• rounds to 3. _____

• is greater than 80. _____

• is less than 31. _____

• is close to $\frac{4}{10}$. _____

FAST Math

Multiply. Circle the product nearest to 100.

47	38	19	436	161	240
× 3	× 2	× 5	× 2	× 6	× 4
___	___	___	___	___	___

Think Tank

Victor went by bus to visit his brother in another state. The bus left at 10:30 A.M. The trip lasted 5 hours. What time was it when Victor arrived?

_____

Show your work in the tank.

Data Place

Jaycee tracked the time she spent on homework.

Display the data in a circle graph. Use a different color for each subject. Label each section. Give the graph a title.

Subject	Part of an Hour
Math	$\frac{2}{12}$
Reading	$\frac{1}{2}$
Science	$\frac{3}{12}$
Spelling	$\frac{1}{12}$

_____

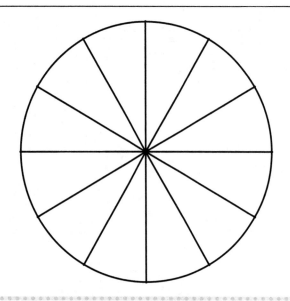

Puzzler

Half a leaf appears on one side of a line of symmetry.

Color squares to complete the rest of the leaf. Keep it symmetrical.

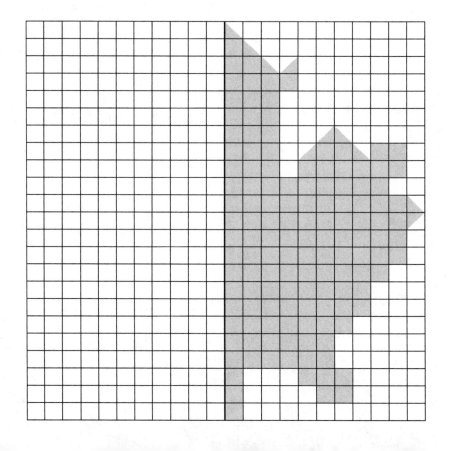

108

Morning Jumpstarts: Math, Grade 3 © 2013 by Scholastic Teaching Resources

Answers

Jumpstart 1
Number Place: (Left to right) 32, 65, 97; 213, 671, 929; 13, 69, 86; 824, 535, 704
Fast Math: (Left to right) 11, 5, 1; 8, 11, 9; 12, 7, 7
Think Tank: Jen
Data Place:

Symbol		Tallies
Sharp	♯	ЖЖ III
Flat	♭	ЖЖ I
Note	♪	ЖЖ ЖЖ I

1. 11 2. 25
Puzzler:

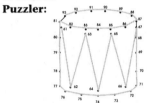

Jumpstart 2
Number Place: (Left to right) 167, 180, 193; 456, 618, 847; 112, 505, 899; 84, 361, 726
Fast Math: (Left to right) 17, 7, 9; 15, 13, 8; 14, 10, 6
Think Tank: wheels; y; responses may vary
Data Place: 1. 24 2. fishing line 3. rod & reel
Puzzler:

8	1	6
3	5	7
4	9	2

Responses may vary.

Jumpstart 3
Number Place: 371, 364, 357; 888, 880, 808; 575, 573, 537
Fast Math: ⑨, 18, 16, ⑦, 8, 14
Think Tank: yes; 75¢ > 67¢
Data Place: 1. theme park 2. 4
3. beach, theme park, jungle, camping
Puzzler: 1. 700 2. 560 3. 138 = 100 + 10 + 10 + 10 + 2 + 2 + 2 + 2

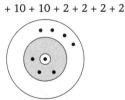

Jumpstart 4
Number Place: 568, 572, 576; 404, 440, 444; 671, 678, 687
Fast Math: (Left to right) 700, 80; 90, 900; 1,300, 60; 1,300 + 60 = 1,360
Think Tank: $1.75
Data Place: 1. guitar 2. 8 3. guitar and violin
Puzzler: 1. 109 2. 45 3. 129 4. 16 5. 115 6. 36

Jumpstart 5
Number Place: (Left to right) 110, 111, 112, 113; 319, 320, 321, 322; 768, 769, 770, 771
Fast Math: odd—33, 41, 125, 747, 929; even—6, 80, 352, 804, 858
Think Tank: 2
Data Place: 1. 22 2. bear 3. 3
Puzzler: Drawings will vary.

Jumpstart 6
Number Place: (Left to right) possible answers: 30, 55; 18, 69; 26 < 74
Fast Math: 52, 54; 89, 91; 115, 117; 622 and others
Think Tank: $1.19 + $1.20 = $2.39
Data Place: 1. 1 ball = 5 students
2. basketball 3. Possible answer: All you need is a field and a ball.
Puzzler:

Jumpstart 7
Number Place:

Thousands	Hundreds	Tens	Ones
2	1	6	1

Fast Math: 11:15, 3:30, 8:45, 12:00; X on 8:45
Think Tank: (32 + 27) – 46 = 13
Data Place:

Range	Tallies	Number
0	ЖЖ I	6
1-2	ЖЖ III	8
3-5	IIII	4
6-8	ЖЖ	5
9 or more	III	3

1. 6 2. 23 3. The 9-or-more row would need 4 tallies and the number 4.
Puzzler: 89, 80, 105

Jumpstart 8
Number Place: (Top to bottom) 599, 899, 99; 400, 800, 1,000
Fast Math: (Left to right) 36, 38, 40, 44; 72, 75, 81, 84; 45, 60, 65, 75
Think Tank: 12; check students' lists or diagrams.
Data Place: parallelogram
Puzzler: 14; answers will vary.

Jumpstart 9
Number Place: (Left to right) 60, 90, 220; 370, 550, 810
Fast Math: (Left to right) 18, 24, 36, 48; 32, 36, 44, 48; 9, 45, 54, 63
Think Tank:

☐ ☐ 🅇 ☐

← ↑ → ↓ ←

☺ ✓ ☹ ✓ ☺

Data Place: 1. 5 2. cooking and science lab 3. arts & crafts and cooking
Puzzler: Cheesetown

Jumpstart 10
Number Place: (Left to right) 100, 900, 400; 700, 300, 900
Fast Math: (Left to right) 28, 35, 49, 56; 16, 40, 48, 64; 11, 55, 66, 88
Think Tank: 14 + 5 = 19
Data Place: 1. 18 2. 6 3. 7 4. 0
Puzzler: 4¢ and 7¢

Jumpstart 11
Number Place: (Left to right) >, >, =; >, <
Fast Math: 5, ⑱ 11, 9, ⑧ 17
Think Tank: 126 inches
Data Place: 1. 14 + 15 2. 3 + 4 + 5 3. 39
4. November 24
Puzzler: 1. 2 and 7 2. 6 and 3

Jumpstart 12
Number Place: 800 + 60 + 3; 900 + 7; 4,000 + 100 + 50 + 2; 2,000 + 10 + 2
Fast Math: 357, 779, ⑥⑦⑧ 879, 789, 958
Think Tank: 104 feet
Data Place: 1. Mercury and Neptune (with 2 votes each); Venus and Saturn (with 3 votes each) 2. Possible answer: because we live here 3. 26
Puzzler:

11	8	3	5	9	14	0	16	8
9	4	13	5	8	13	10	8	7
2	3	7	10	11	9	6	8	9
18	9	9	6	3	4	5	9	16
7	9	16	4	8	12	11	17	4

Jumpstart 13
Number Place: one thousand two hundred ninety-six; eight thousand seventy-five; three thousand three hundred sixty-four; twenty-four thousand, six hundred eighty-nine
Fast Math: 424, ⑦①③ 112, 246, 622, 220
Think Tank: 107 feet
Data Place: 1. five-minute break, maybe to switch gears, get materials, go to another room 2. lunch and recess
3. longest: reading; shortest: class meeting
Puzzler: 1. 34 2. 41 3. 37 4. 41 5. 36 6. 52

Jumpstart 14
Number Place: 864
Fast Math: 97, ⑧① 939, 1,259, 739, 1,179
Think Tank: 45 beads; multiply 9 × 5
Data Place: 1. $1.00 2. $.98 3. 1 marker; 4¢ more 4. 8
Puzzler: 1. 17 2. 8 3. 12 4. 25

Answers

Jumpstart 15
Number Place:

Pig	Dollars	Dimes	Pennies
1			7
2	1	7	5
3		5	9

Fast Math: 47, 24, (419) 262, 250, 43
Think Tank: 4 equal teams; no but 3 kids can be substitutes.
Data Place: Answers will vary; check students' graphs for accuracy.
Puzzler: (Left to right) 8**66** – 3**48**; 1**23** + 4**68** = 5**91**; **763** – **109**; **385** + **515**; **936** – **274**

Jumpstart 16
Number Place: $.42, $.80, $.11, $.06
Fast Math: 183, 157, 728, 1455, (930) 824
Think Tank: 91 more miles
Data Place: Answers will vary; check students' Venn diagrams.
Puzzler: Answers will vary; check students' designs.

Jumpstart 17
Number Place: $1.37, $4.59, $6.00, $2.81
Fast Math: 328, 365, (274), 283, 389, (544)
Think Tank: Taye is 10; Femi is 7.
Data Place: 1. Cedar 2. 38 3. Elm and Pine
Puzzler: The path below shows 570.

Jumpstart 18
Number Place: (Left to right) 40¢, 50¢, 80¢; 40¢, 70¢, 10¢
Fast Math: 777, 344, 413, 291, 316, (29)
Think Tank: 3½ hours
Data Place: 1. different after-school activities 2. play sports 3. do homework
Puzzler: 18; by different-size rectangles

Jumpstart 19
Number Place: (Left to right) $1, $2, $4; $4, $5, $7
Fast Math: (139) 137, (139) 1,465, 1,627, 1,728
Think Tank: 46 meters; twice length + twice width
Data Place: 1. 47 more seats in main floor 2. 2nd Balcony 3. Main Floor Center
Puzzler:

Jumpstart 20
Number Place: $9.75, $3.60, $5.03, $8.00
Fast Math: 400, 1,003, 1,171, (1,412) 666, 966
Think Tank: all but the markers; $4.93
Data Place: 1. 4 votes 2. lemon: 2; peach: 14 3. 8
Puzzler:

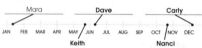

1. $70 2. $1 + $2 + $4 + $8 + $16 + $32 + $64 = $125 3. No, you'd only earn $63.50.

Jumpstart 21
Number Place: 920, 900; 860, 900; 350, 300
Fast Math: (Left to right) sample answers: 600, 100; 300, 400
Think Tank: 14 + 20 = 34 legs
Data Place:

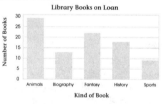

1. Keith and Dave 2. Nanci and Carly 3. Mara is the oldest; Carly is the youngest.
Puzzler: Sample answers: 3 tennis balls in a can; 4 legs on a cow; 5 fingers; 6 legs on an ant; 7 days in a week; 8 legs on an octopus; 9 players on a baseball team; 10 toes

Jumpstart 22
Number Place: (Left to right) sample answers: 220, 450; 780, 580; 925, 250
Fast Math: (Top to bottom) 18, 24, 30, 36; 21, 28, 35, 42
Think Tank: 27; 3 × (5 + 4)
Data Place:

1. 5 2. I used number sense.
Puzzler: sternutation

Jumpstart 23
Number Place: 392, 1,284, 451, 660
Fast Math: (Left to right) 12, 20, 14; 7, 21, (18) (18) 24, 16
Think Tank: 44°F; 72 – 28
Data Place:

1. Students might live in a warm climate.
2. jump rope and scooter
Puzzler: 1. 444 + 666 = 1,110 **2.** 39 × 3 = 117 **3.** 828 – 282 = 546 **4.** 55 ÷ 5 = 11

Jumpstart 24
Number Place: (Top to bottom) 809, 5,531, 525, 2,174
Fast Math: (Left to right) 25, 32, (36) 42, (36) 48; 27, 35, 49
Think Tank: 80 square feet; 10 × 8 = 80
Data Place: 1. $1.39 2. catnip toy and flea collar 3. $1.25
Puzzler: 253 + 255 = 508; 755 – 85 = 670

Jumpstart 25
Number Place: 7,601, 7,160, 7,106, 7,061; 5,985, 5,958, 5,859, 5,589; 3,241, 3,214, 3,142, 3,124
Fast Math: (Left to right) 64, 56, 72; 54, 42, 56; 63, 54, 81; circle 6 × 9 and 9 × 6; 8 × 7 and 7 × 8.
Think Tank: 22 units
Data Place: 1. (3, 2) 2. (2, 4) 3. (0, 1) 4. (1, 3) 5. pond
Puzzler:

2	9	4
7	5	3
6	1	8

Jumpstart 26
Number Place: 8,057, 8,570, 8,705, 8,750; 6,293, 6,392, 6,923, 6,932; 4,104, 4,140, 4401, 4410
Fast Math: (Left to right) 80, 280, 70; 120, 200, 160; 270, 180, (450)
Think Tank: 2 quarters, 2 dimes, 1 penny
Data Place:

Key	Tally	Number
												10
							5
											9
									7

There are 31 computer keys in all.
Puzzler: perimeter = 20 units; area = 9 square units

Jumpstart 27
Number Place:

0.1	0.3		0.7	0.9

0.0   0.2   0.4   0.5   0.6   0.8   1.0

Fast Math: (Left to right) 1,800, 3,600, 2,400; 800, 2,500, (1,400) 2,100, 1,600, 900
Think Tank: Thursday, Friday, Saturday
Data Place: 1. Toast and Maple 2. Sienna; 7
Puzzler:

Jumpstart 28
Number Place: (Left to right) 0.3, 0.2; 0.6, 0.8, 0.7; 0.9, (0.5) 0.4
Fast Math: (Left to right) 3, 7, 9; 6, 5, 4; 6, 7, 9; circled quotients will vary.
Think Tank: The snail will get out in 6 days.
Data Place:

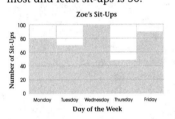

Puzzler: polygon; trapezoid

Jumpstart 29
Number Place: (Left to right) $\frac{1}{10}$, $\frac{2}{10}$; $\frac{3}{10}$, $\frac{6}{10}$, $\frac{9}{10}$; $\frac{9}{10}$, $\frac{4}{10}$, $\frac{7}{10}$; greatest decimal is $\frac{9}{10}$
Fast Math: (Left to right) 1, 2, 8; 6, 7, 4; 4, 8, 1
Think Tank: ahead—8; behind—18; 8 + 18 + 1 = 27
Data Place: 1. cabbage and onions **2.** lima beans
Puzzler: 1. 73¢ **2.** 65¢

Jumpstart 30
Number Place: (Left to right) >, >, <; <, <, >
Fast Math: (Left to right) 4, 6, 6; 5, 4, 7; 8, 9, 9
Think Tank: 18 goals
Data Place: The difference between most and least sit-ups is 50.

Puzzler: Sample answers—red (3, 1) (2, 4) (2, 2); saw (4, 3) (3, 2) (3, 5); Mario (6, 3) (3, 2) (3, 1) (1, 1) (5, 4); cake (3, 0) (3, 2) (0, 4) (2, 4)

Jumpstart 31
Number Place: (Left to right) 0.2, 0.4, 0.6, 0.9; 0.1, 0.3, 0.7, 0.8; 0.8, 0.6, 0.4, 0.1; 0.9, 0.7, 0.5, 0.3
Fast Math: (Left to right) 2, 9, 8; 4, 3, 8; 6, 5, 7; answers will vary.
Think Tank: 50 blocks; (4 + 21) × 2
Data Place: 1. 4 **2.** Lincoln, 65 **3.** Eagle and Flag **4.** $4.50
Puzzler: Sample answer—

	200	
100	500	400
	300	

Jumpstart 32
Number Place:

Fast Math: (Left to right) 72, 30, 49; 56, 0, 28; 42, 3, 48
Think Tank: $\frac{2}{8}$
Data Place:

Range	Tallies	Number
1–3	‖‖ I	6
4–6	‖‖ ‖‖ ‖‖ ‖‖ ‖‖ ‖‖ ‖‖ III	38
7–9	‖‖ ‖‖ ‖‖ ‖‖ ‖‖ ‖‖ IIII	34
10–12	‖‖ ‖‖ ‖‖ II	17
13 or More	‖‖ II	7

1. 4–6 **2.** Answers will vary. **3.** 7–9
Puzzler:

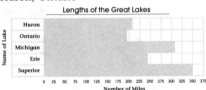

Jumpstart 33
Number Place: (Left to right) 0.30, 0.72; 0.63, 0.81, 0.94; 0.29, 0.05, (0.50)
Fast Math: (Left to right) 9, 8, 6; 7, 9, 0; 7, 6, 9
Think Tank: 3¾ hours
Data Place: Superior, Michigan, Erie, Huron, Ontario

Lengths of the Great Lakes

Puzzler: Tilt tail down to form top of *new* head; reposition 1 toothpick from *old* head to form rest of *new* head.

Note: new tail will be pointing down.

Jumpstart 34
Number Place: (Left to right) $\frac{3}{100}$, $\frac{26}{100}$; $\frac{75}{100}$, $\frac{61}{100}$, $\frac{98}{100}$; $\frac{40}{100}$, $\frac{52}{100}$, $\frac{86}{100}$
Fast Math: 5 + 8 = 13, 8 + 5 = 13, 13 − 8 = 5, 13 − 5 = 8; 7 × 8 = 56, 8 × 7 = 56, 56 ÷ 7 = 8, 56 ÷ 8 = 7
Think Tank: 1.9 kilograms
Data Place: 1. Colorado and Trinity **2.** 700 miles **3.** Red
Puzzler:

Jumpstart 35
Number Place: (Left to right) <, >, <; >, =, >
Fast Math: (Left to right) 8, 24, 48; 27, 35, 0; 14, 0, 60; circle 9 × 7 × 0 and 5 × 0 × 8.
Think Tank: 3.57 minutes
Data Place: 1. 17 **2.** 4 **3.** 6 **4.** 2 **5.** sample answer: how many students missed more than 3 words
Puzzler: 4 insects and 3 spiders

Jumpstart 36
Number Place: 0.12, 0.35, 0.49; 0.2, 0.49, 0.63; 0.38, 0.4, 0.43; 0.06, 0.7, 0.75
Fast Math: 10:17, 2:53, 6:08; 1:32; X on 2:53
Think Tank: 28 square units; count all shaded squares.
Data Place: 1. 17 and 18 **2.** 9 and 10 **3.** April 28 **4.** Friday
Puzzler: Initial input may vary; answer shows age and number of people in family.

Jumpstart 37
Number Place: 4.05, 4.5, 4.75, 4.98
Fast Math: $.77, $1.46, $6.30
Think Tank: 91 years old
Data Place: 1. 109 **2.** balloons and costumes **3.** 16
Puzzler: Check that students connected only the multiples of 4. The picture is a helicopter.

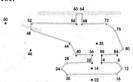

Jumpstart 38
Number Place: 0.7, 3.5, 0.45, 9.11
Fast Math: $9.10, $2.83, $8.92, $2.38, ($8.16) $3.29
Think Tank: 3,545 more visitors in 1982
Data Place: 1. *Space Racers* **2.** *Zebra Force* **3.** *Action Alley* and *Space Racers* **4.** *Time Travel* or *Zebra Force*; the movie starting times are closest to 1:50.
Puzzler: Answers will vary; check students' designs.

Jumpstart 39
Number Place: (Left to right) eight tenths, forty-two hundredths; one and one tenth, three and fifty-nine hundredths
Fast Math: Check that students shaded $\frac{1}{3}$, $\frac{3}{5}$, $\frac{5}{6}$ and $\frac{1}{2}$
Think Tank: 168 teeth; find 42 × 4
Data Place: 1. $12 **2.** 5 **3.** 2 tomato plants; 6¢ more
Puzzler: Sample answers—**1.** 3:00 and 9:00 **2.** 6:00 and 12:00 **3.** 3:00 and 9:00 **4.** 12:00 and 6:30

Answers

Jumpstart 40
Number Place: 0.3 + 0.08, 1.0 + 0.4, 2.0 + 0.06, 7.0 + 0.7 + 0.07
Fast Math: $\frac{1}{4}$, $\frac{2}{3}$ ($\frac{3}{6}$) $\frac{2}{5}$
Think Tank: Muffy is 16.
Data Place:

Vowel	Tally	Number
a	I	1
e	ﬀHL	5
i	III	3
o	II	2
u	III	3

One fewer *e* and one fewer *i*; might add a row for *y*, which is sometimes a vowel.
Puzzler:

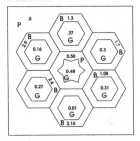

Jumpstart 41
Number Place: (Left to right) $.55, 5 nickels; 11 dimes, 5 quarters; $.80, $1.04
Fast Math:

$\frac{0}{8}$ $\frac{1}{8}$ $\frac{2}{8}$ $\frac{3}{8}$ $\frac{4}{8}$ $\frac{5}{8}$ $\frac{6}{8}$ $\frac{7}{8}$ $\frac{8}{8}$

Think Tank: Lu has 29 ducks; Pia has 22 ducks; use "guess and test."
Data Place:

Thu / Fri / Sat / Sun
0 50 100 150 200 250 300 350 400

Puzzler:

82	59	52	48
18	41	73	96
26	74	37	4

Jumpstart 42
Number Place: (Left to right) sample answers: 0.2, 0.75; 7.7, 7.77; 2.4, 2.88; 10.3, 10.61
Fast Math: $\frac{2}{4}$, $\frac{5}{10}$, $\frac{3}{6}$, $\frac{4}{8}$, $\frac{6}{12}$, $\frac{10}{20}$; $\frac{1}{2}$
Think Tank: 515 passengers
Data Place: multiples of 4—4, 8, 16, 20, 28, 32, 40; multiples of 6—6, 18, 30, 42, 54; multiples of both—12, 24, 36,
Puzzler: 1. 8 and 7 **2.** 10 and 5 **3.** 10 and 4 **4.** 9 and 9

Jumpstart 43
Number Place: 9,762, 2,679, 9,762, 9,627
Fast Math: (Left to right) 5, 8, 2, 6, 10, 3; 4, 1, 7, 9, 12, 16
Think Tank: 20 mugs
Data Place: 1. orange **2.** $\frac{1}{10}$ **3.** apple **4.** 40
Puzzler: 1. F **2.** B **3.** R **4.** M **5.** Z **6.** G **7.** C **8.** K

Jumpstart 44
Number Place: (Left to right) <, >, =; <, <, >
Fast Math: $2\frac{1}{3}$, $1\frac{4}{5}$, $3\frac{1}{2}$, $2\frac{3}{4}$
Think Tank: about 1,600
Data Place:

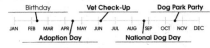

1. Birthday, Adoption Day, and Vet Check-Up **2.** about 2 months **3.** National Dog Day
Puzzler: 19 × 4 = 76; 999 ÷ 3 = 333

Jumpstart 45
Number Place: 30,868, 23,689, 48,732, 70,320
Fast Math: pint, 4, 1, gallon
Think Tank: $\frac{9}{10}$
Data Place:

Place to Swim	Tally	Number
Creek	ﬀHL IIII	9
Lake	ﬀHL ﬀHL ﬀHL III	18
Ocean	ﬀHL II	7
Pool	ﬀHL ﬀHL ﬀHL ﬀHL ﬀHL	25

Puzzler: 1,3 and 4 are *gloinks*. A *gloink* is a closed figure (polygon) with no curves.

Jumpstart 46
Number Place: $7.40, $7; $1.30, $1; $6.90, $7; $5.00, $5
Fast Math: yards, miles, feet, inches
Think Tank: $\frac{3}{8}$
Data Place: Outcomes and observations will vary; check students' line plots.
Puzzler:

2	1	4	3
4	3	1	2
3	4	2	1
1	2	3	4

Jumpstart 47
Number Place: 785.64, 740.26, 623.45, 604.78, 435.09
Fast Math: 1. 2 cm **2.** 3 cm **3.** 4 cm **4.** 1 cm
Think Tank: 54 books; 33 magazines
Data Place: 1. $4 back **2.** Orders and costs will vary. **3.** Yes, there will be 25¢ left.
Puzzler: divisible by 3 (red) 21, 6, 3, 18, 9, 27; by 4 (blue) 4, 8, 32, 16, 28; by 5 (green) 5, 25, 35, 50, 10

Jumpstart 48
Number Place: 3,951
Fast Math: (Left to right) 96, 82, 88, 608, 770, (168)
Think Tank: 108 months old
Data Place: 1. Sarasota **2.** Key West and Tampa **3.** Sarasota and Tampa **4.** 10
Puzzler: Check that students' drawings show the given area in each grid.

Jumpstart 49
Number Place: 4,300, 4,000; 9,200, 9,000; 6,700, 7,000; 8,100, 8,000
Fast Math: (Left to right) 24, (13) 22, 230, 100, 312
Think Tank: 27 cubes; 3 layers of 9 cubes each
Data Place: 1. 8:55 **2.** 9:30 **3.** 9:55 **4.** Drake Rd.
Puzzler:

Jumpstart 50
Number Place: sample answers: 38.0, 3.08, 80.3, 30.8, 0.38
Fast Math: 141, 76, (95) 872, 966, 960
Think Tank: 3:30 P.M.
Data Place:

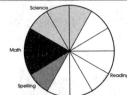

How Long Jaycee Spent on Homework
(Science, Math, Spelling, Reading)

graph titles will vary; possible answer: How Long Jaycee Spent on Homework
Puzzler:

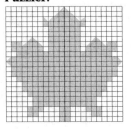

112